Bullying Today

BULLYING TODAY

Bullet Points and Best Practices

Justin W. Patchin

Sameer Hinduja

CORWIN
A SAGE Publishing Company

FOR INFORMATION:

Corwin

A SAGE Company

2455 Teller Road

Thousand Oaks, California 91320

(800) 233-9936

www.corwin.com

SAGE Publications Ltd.

1 Oliver's Yard

55 City Road

London EC1Y 1SP

United Kingdom

SAGE Publications India Pvt. Ltd.

B 1/I 1 Mohan Cooperative Industrial Area

Mathura Road, New Delhi 110 044

India

SAGE Publications Asia-Pacific Pte. Ltd.

3 Church Street

#10-04 Samsung Hub

Singapore 049483

Printed in the United States of America

Library of Congress Cataloging-in-Publication Data

Names: Patchin, Justin W., 1977- author. | Hinduja, Sameer, 1978- author.

Title: Bullying today : bullet points and best practices / Justin W. Patchin, Sameer Hinduja.

Description: Thousand Oaks, California : Corwin, a Sage Company, [2016] | Includes bibliographical references and index.

Identifiers: LCCN 2015048523 | ISBN 9781506335971 (pbk. : alk. paper)

Subjects: LCSH: Bullying in schools. | Bullying in schools—Prevention. | Cyberbullying. | Cyberbullying—Prevention.

Classification: LCC LB3013.3 .P375 2016 | DDC 371.5/8—dc23 LC record available at http://lccn.loc.gov/2015048523

This book is printed on acid-free paper.

Acquisitions Editor: Ariel Bartlett

Editorial Assistant: Andrew Olson

Production Editor: Amy Schroller

Copy Editor: Melinda Masson

Typesetter: C&M Digitals (P) Ltd.

Proofreader: Ellen Howard

Indexer: Sheila Bodell

Cover Designer: Candice Harman

SUSTAINABLE FORESTRY INITIATIVE

Certified Chain of Custody
Promoting Sustainable Forestry
www.sfiprogram.org
SFI-01268

SFI label applies to text stock

16 17 18 19 20 10 9 8 7 6 5 4 3 2 1

CONTENTS

PREFACE

While adolescent bullying remains a hot-button issue in schools and communities, adults tasked with addressing these behaviors continue to clamor for research-based guidance on exactly what to do. Those who experience bullying struggle emotionally, relationally, and academically (as do those who target them), and often feel helpless even though they are desperately looking for support. Frankly, we're all too familiar with the tragic stories of students who take the most extreme measures to escape the relentless abuse they face. Quite simply, more needs to be done.

We've devoted all of our professional lives to illuminating the causes and consequences of teen bullying. We've been studying these behaviors (with a particular emphasis on cyberbullying) since about 2002. As you can imagine, a lot has changed over that time. We've formally surveyed over 15,000 middle and high school students from schools large and small all across the United States. And we've sat down and chatted with countless others. We also work very closely with educators in school settings and parents in communities to keep informed on their experiences, successes, and struggles wrestling with the misuse of smartphones and social media.

As action researchers and writers, we aim that our work impacts the lives and efforts of those on the front lines. That is, we don't just publish academic articles in peer-reviewed journals for our university colleagues (though we do that too!). We write for educator and parenting publications. We've written several books for adults and students. But the book in front of you is something different than what we have typically written in the past. Like all of our work, *Bullying Today* is grounded in research and guided by the practical experiences of those who confront bullying on a daily basis. However, rather than providing you with six to eight long, dense chapters jam-packed with weighty information, we've created a collection of shorter chapters that all pointedly address a particular problem or perspective. Many began as blog posts on our website (cyberbullying.org), which have been updated and expanded while maintaining their succinctness and readability. Instead of comprehensive and formalized prose, we opted for easily digestible informational nuggets presented in a journalistic, conversational style. In speaking with educators and others who follow our work all around the United States (and abroad), we've come to learn that they appreciate the way we write on our blog, and value our relatable and research-informed perspectives.

ORGANIZATION OF THE BOOK

Our book is subdivided into five main sections. The first—*Defining Bullying: What It Is and What It Isn't*—presents a discussion of exactly what constitutes this misbehavior and, consequently, what does not. This is essential because labeling every instance of drama or conflict between youths as "bullying" is detrimental to our ability to devote time and energy to serious issues, and also preempts the opportunity to show kids how to solve some of their own relational problems. Next, we explore research in *Bullying by the Numbers: What We Know* to provide a baseline for what is known about bullying in order to clarify perspectives of its frequency and impact, and to correct misperceptions that affect the way society approaches and responds to it. The third subsection, *The Lowdown on Laws Related to Bullying*, focuses on the relevance of the law. With all 50 U.S. states having some kind of bullying statute in place, it is important for educators to know exactly what they need to consider when addressing these behaviors in their schools. Educators from outside the United States can also benefit from the legislative lessons learned here. Furthermore, it is useful to understand the limitations of law and formal policy in actually preventing repeated peer harassment among a population of vulnerable and impressionable youth.

The fourth and fifth sections of the book help equip school personnel with both the knowledge and the strategies to capably deal with bullying. In *Preventing Bullying Before It Starts: What You Can Do*, we discuss the role of student assemblies, student advisory boards, how to create a kindness movement to combat cruelty and hate among the student body, and other related programming educators can immediately implement at little to no cost. In *Rational Responses to Bullying: What Works and What Doesn't*, we cover a number of key subjects: for instance, we clarify how youth-serving adults can promptly address instances of online bullying through anonymous reporting systems, device policies, and formal or informal intervention.

Almost every single day, we are contacted by an educator, a parent, or another adult who works with youth and is looking for solutions to the bullying problem. While there simply doesn't exist a quick and easy fix, there are certain incontrovertible points that adults need to know when it comes to identifying bullying and reducing its negative impact. We've distilled those best practices for you in this book, and sought to present them in a concise, memorable, and valuable way that you can reference as needed. We will continue to blog regularly about these issues at cyberbullying.org and hope that you'll follow our most recent musing there. Most importantly, we hope that you'll reach out if you need additional assistance (patchin@ cyberbullying.org or hinduja@cyberbullying.org). Our first and foremost goal is to be there for you, so that you can be there for others.

Acknowledgments

This book would not have been possible without the assistance of a number of important individuals in our personal and professional lives. First, we are both grateful to have supportive families who have cared for, encouraged, and inspired us over the years. Their love and affirmation has sustained us through the long hours of research and writing. We gratefully acknowledge the Office of Research and Sponsored Programs at the University of Wisconsin–Eau Claire and the Division of Research at Florida Atlantic University for their support of our research presented throughout this book.

We would also like to convey appreciation to our professional colleagues who labor alongside us to better understand adolescent bullying behaviors. We are most grateful to those who provided valuable counsel and critical feedback throughout the years, including Emily Bazelon, Michele Borba, Anne Collier, Stan Davis, Elizabeth Englander, Darren Laur, Amanda Lenhart, Trudy Ludwig, Larry Magid, Charisse Nixon, Sue Scheff, Rachel Simmons, Deb Temkin, Nancy Willard, and Rosalind Wiseman. For them, and for all who have been affected by bullying in all its forms, we offer this book as well as our commitment to continue this vital work. Finally, we would like to thank God for giving us the opportunities and abilities to study this problem and contribute to its understanding.

We would also like to thank the staff at Corwin and SAGE Publishing for their expert guidance throughout this process. We are indebted to Ariel Bartlett for helping us to bring this project to fruition. We also thank Melinda Masson for clarifying the meaning of our words while keeping our respective voices. We were also fortunate to have several blind reviewers whose suggestions contributed to a tighter and more comprehensive work.

PUBLISHER'S ACKNOWLEDGMENTS

Corwin would like to thank the following reviewers for their editorial insight and guidance:

Deb Bible
Educational Consultant
Hanover Park, IL

Dr. Vera J. Blake
Educational Consultant
V.J. Blake & Associates, Inc.
Dumfries, VA

Charla Bunker
Literacy Specialist
Great Falls High School
Great Falls, MT

Avis Canty
Instructional Technology Facilitator
Greenville County School District
Greenville, SC

Tamara Daugherty
Art Teacher
Lakeville Elementary
Apopka, FL

Joy Rose
High School Principal (Retired)
Westerville City Schools
Westerville, OH

ABOUT THE AUTHORS

 **Justin W. Patchin,** PhD, is a professor of criminal justice at the University of Wisconsin–Eau Claire.

Sameer Hinduja, PhD, is a professor of criminology and criminal justice at Florida Atlantic University.

Since 2002, Dr. Patchin and Dr. Hinduja have been exploring the online behaviors of adolescents, including cyberbullying, social networking, and sexting. They are the authors of six other books on the topic of cyberbullying,  including *School Climate 2.0: Preventing Cyberbullying and Sexting One Classroom at a Time* and *Bullying Beyond the Schoolyard: Preventing and Responding to Cyberbullying* (2nd edition) (both from Corwin). They travel across the United States and abroad training educators, parents, teens, and others on how to keep youth safe online. They codirect the Cyberbullying Research Center (cyberbullying .org) that serves as an information clearinghouse for those interested in learning more about cyberbullying and what they can do about it.

PART I

DEFINING BULLYING

What It Is and What It Isn't

1

BULLIES OR BEST FRIENDS?

The Challenge of Interpreting Interpersonal Relationships

Justin W. Patchin

The other night, I found myself in the proximity of a group of guys who were playing a game together. As they played, they talked—about sports and relationships and game strategy and many other topics that you might imagine would come up among a group of young men. From my eavesdropping, it seemed that they were all longtime acquaintances. But it was also evident that there were some major power dynamics at play within this bunch. One or two members dominated the conversation, while a few others sat back and focused their energy on the game rather than the gossip.

From an outsider's perspective, some of the interpersonal interactions could easily be characterized as bullying. To be clear, there wasn't any *physical* bullying going on, but I witnessed a lot of name calling, degradation, humiliation, and exclusion. Curse words were cast like paint in a Jackson Pollock piece. Bad gameplay was harshly criticized, and one or another's masculinity was regularly challenged based on what was said (or not said) and done (or not done). For me, a social scientist who explores these behaviors empirically on a daily basis, this represented a petri dish of the real-world manifestations of bullying that I regularly see in my data.

One of the things I noticed was that while no one was immune from attack, certain targets appeared to be favored. One among the group seemed to be persecuted more than any of the others. He had a way about him that seemed to attract ridicule and reproach. He behaved unconventionally (in the game and, based on what I overheard, in the "real world"), and was clearly lacking in social competence. I also noticed that the older members of this group seemed to be revered to an extent among the younger ones, and therefore their aggressive behaviors were often mimicked by the younger ones in an attempt to fit in (and perhaps also to avoid becoming browbeaten themselves).

But I have a confession to make. The interactions I have just described can be best characterized as "participant observation," rather than purely observation, because *I was a member of this group and we were all adults*. In fact, I use the term *young men* very loosely when referring to those assembled because, at "30-something," I was the youngest of the group. The relationships and interchanges portrayed represented the dynamics not among a group of apathetic adolescents playing a multiplayer online game like *World of Warcraft* or *League of Legends*, but rather among those of mostly white-collar academics in my monthly poker game.

It struck me as I contemplated my terrible cards that night that there is not all that much difference between the way we treat our best friends and the way we treat our worst enemies. Taking our behavior out of context, an outside observer would surely have believed that bullying was occurring within our group. The actions expressed included all of the classic definitional characteristics: repeated, apparently intentional harassment (meanness, cruelty, etc.) carried out by those with perceived or actual power (social status, academic reputation, etc.) against targets in a way that allowed for little defense.

Most of the comments were accompanied by laughter from many in the group, including the one being roasted, which may have masked the maliciousness of the back-and-forth. But we've learned through our conversations with teens who bully that a lot of bullying behaviors are done by young people who think they are just joking around. So I actually found myself wondering, after particularly punishing digs, whether some of the comments made that night had crossed an imperceptible line. And if this boundary is difficult for adults to identify, how can we expect teens to know when something goes too far? This is especially challenging because often-times targets of ridicule do in fact respond with laughter publicly—in an effort to save face—while privately they are really hurt by what was said.

I also reflected on this as it relates to my research. As academics, we like to debate the best way to define bullying—or at least discuss the limitations of defining it in certain ways. If I were to survey my card-playing

> If the boundary for bullying is often difficult for adults to identify, how can we expect teens to know when something is taken too far?

colleagues about their experiences with peer abuse by asking them, for example, if anyone has ever "said something mean to them" or "made fun of them in front of others" (two indicators included in the commonly used Olweus bully/victim questionnaire[1]), they would have to say yes just based on how they were treated by their friends that night. But is it accurate to say that they were *bullied*? Often, typical research approaches don't allow scholars to accurately distinguish between good-natured ribbing and malevolent meanness. As I will discuss in more detail in Chapter 3, I don't believe that *bullying* can be done unintentionally. Even though someone's feelings can certainly be hurt without intent, bullying by definition is deliberate. That said, whether hurtful actions qualify as bullying by academic standards or not is beside the point. If we are treating people in ways that make them uncomfortable, humiliated, excluded, or hurt in any possible way, then we should stop. But how do we know if our comments are being received in that light? And when they are delivered from a distance, as online comments are, determining their hurtful impact can be extremely difficult, no matter the age of the sender and receiver.

I doubt that most people would categorize the behaviors I have described from my poker game as bullying. But are we, and is research, able to tell the difference?

QUESTIONS FOR REFLECTION

Is it possible to write a policy or design a research study that accurately distinguishes playful banter among friends from bullying? Have you ever been really hurt by something a friend did or said, even though you know he or she probably didn't intend it to be hurtful?

2

DISTINGUISHING BULLYING FROM OTHER HURTFUL BEHAVIORS

Justin W. Patchin

In Chapter 1, I wrote about the difficulty in determining when *mean* behavior crosses the line and becomes *bullying* behavior. I also discussed the challenge for researchers in trying to quantify the difference. In this chapter, I'd like to talk about why it is important to establish such a line.

Academics often debate how best to define bullying. I've never been one to get too caught up in the definitional debate because I feel that whether a behavior meets someone's artificially created criteria for bullying or not really doesn't matter all that much. Admittedly, *as a researcher*, I am frustrated by the myriad ways bullying is defined, primarily because these discrepancies make comparisons across different studies difficult. But just that something satisfies one scholar's standards for being classified as bullying is not what's most important. We should focus instead on addressing the behavior for what it is. If one student called another student a mean name, or posted an embarrassing picture of another online, or pushed someone in the hallway, it should be addressed. Maybe these incidents constitute bullying, and maybe they do not. Either way, they need to be dealt with immediately and appropriately.

I've begun to shift my thinking a bit when it comes to deliberations about the definition of bullying. Don't get me wrong—I still believe that educators, parents, and other adults who work with youth need to deal with all forms of interpersonal harm when confronted with them. But for a number of reasons, we do need to draw a line in the sand for when a behavior (or series of behaviors) reaches the level of being accurately characterized as bullying. Below I discuss some of these and offer what I believe to be the most important distinguishing features of bullying.

NOT ALL INTERPERSONAL ADOLESCENT HURTFUL BEHAVIORS ARE BULLYING

Many kids say or do mean things to others, but the vast majority of them do not bully. Calling all harmful behaviors bullying discounts the experiences of those who are bullied. As Emily Bazelon has argued, "when every bad thing that happens to children gets called bullying, we end up with misleading narratives that obscure other distinct forms of harm."[2] Under most definitions, bullying is much worse than simply being mistreated, pushed, or generally made fun of. To be sure, the difference might simply be in the frequency with which one is targeted. Being pushed in a onetime altercation with a former friend might not be bullying, whereas being pushed by this same person several times over several days, weeks, or months may be. *Frequency does matter.* For example, we were contacted awhile back by an adult who recalled his experience of being bullied from over a half century earlier. He wasn't physically harmed at all, but the names he was incessantly called created psychological scars that never fully healed. Without a doubt, being targeted over and over again, even with relatively mild forms of mistreatment, eventually takes a toll.

> Many kids say or do mean things to others, but the vast majority of them do not bully.

Likewise, calling all harmful behaviors bullying may diminish the seriousness of incidents that are much worse than the term conveys. For example, if a student is attacked on the playground in a onetime incident, this is not bullying. Even if the student is physically beaten so severely that she ends up in the hospital for a week, it's still not bullying. It is an assault, and should be identified and treated as such. If the assault is linked to other behaviors previously or subsequently perpetrated by the aggressor toward the target, then perhaps it is accurate to define the trajectory of events as *bullying*. In isolation, a onetime act—no matter how serious—is not bullying.[3]

IMPLICATIONS FOR SCHOOLS

Using bullying to describe all variations of student-on-student harm also has consequences for schools. Recently passed laws in some states require educators to take certain steps once a behavior is classified as bullying.[4] Well intentioned or not, these laws force schools into following specific and time-consuming procedures. For example, school administrators in New Jersey are required to initiate a formal investigation within one school day of receiving any report of bullying.[5] The school superintendent must be briefed within two school days. The investigation must be completed within ten school days and include a written report of the incident. The results of the investigation must be reported to the school board at its next regularly scheduled meeting.

All of this is well and good, and schools would love to direct this much attention to any problems that arise. The challenge is that they simply have not been given adequate resources to accomplish any of this effectively. It would take an army of administrators to follow through on all of these procedures if every rude, annoying, or even hurtful incident were classified as bullying. There simply aren't enough hours in the day.

Moreover, schools are increasingly being judged by the number of bullying reports received each year. All reports of bullying in New Jersey schools, for example, must be submitted to the state department of education, which will then "grade each school for the purpose of assessing its effort" to address these problems. As a result, some school administrators might be encouraged to dismiss bona fide incidents of bullying—if their numbers start to get too high—for fear of their school being labeled a "bad" one. My question is, if a school shows a high number of bullying reports or interventions, is that a good thing or a bad thing? I mean, it's nice to know that students are comfortable reporting the bullying and that schools are taking it seriously by documenting and conducting a formal investigation. But at what point do high numbers cause us to be concerned? In fact, I personally would be more uneasy about a school that reported *zero* bullying incidents than one that reported quite a few.

ALTERNATIVES TO CALLING EVERYTHING BULLYING

To counter some of these concerns, some have advocated for abolishing the use of the term *bullying* altogether and instead suggested that terms such as *harassment* or *drama* are more appropriate.[6] Neither of these alternatives really solves any of the previously described problems. In many legal circles, for instance, *harassment* is a specific term reserved for mistreatment related to one's protected status (based on sex, race, color, national origin, disability, and actual or perceived sexual orientation).[7] If a heterosexual boy posts an embarrassing picture on Instagram of another heterosexual boy, is it harassment? Not by some legal standards.

And calling all teen disagreements drama also dilutes the problem. To be sure, there is a lot of background noise in schools these days that could be classified as drama. Being upset with your best friend because of some actual or perceived affront is drama. So is refusing to talk to your sister because she ate the last Pop-Tart for breakfast. Most of what teens would call drama would not fall under most definitions of bullying. Nor should it. As danah boyd and Alice Marwick have found in their interviews with youth, "teenagers say drama when they want to diminish the importance of something."[8] Referring to a bullying incident as drama allows the aggressor to neutralize his or her role in the harm. If everyone does these kinds of things, and if drama is just an everyday part of life for teens, then it isn't that big a deal or worth focusing on.

Bullying is *deliberate, repeated harm inflicted by one or more toward another who is unable to effectively defend him- or herself.* Accidentally hurting someone's feelings is not bullying (for more on this, see Chapter 3). Yes, it sometimes can be difficult to determine the intent of a person causing harm, but repeated hurtful actions, especially after the bully has been made aware that what he or she did was wrong, are a clear indication of intent. Similarly, hurting someone one time in an isolated incident is not bullying, although if there is a threat of repetition, the behavior may qualify. Also, posting something online might be a onetime behavior, but the fact that the content is repeatedly accessible means the victimization is likely to continue. And if the hurtful behaviors do continue, or if a student tells you that he is being bullied, then clearly he does not have the ability to defend himself.

> Bullying is deliberate, repeated harm inflicted by one or more toward another who is unable to effectively defend him- or herself.

Recognizing that not all hurtful behavior is bullying is an important step toward addressing this problem, as it becomes perhaps slightly more manageable. My criteria offered above are just some issues to consider when trying to differentiate bullying from other behaviors. You might have some ideas of your own, and I encourage you to discuss them. While we might not come to complete agreement on this, we can work together to prevent and effectively respond to all forms of adolescent interpersonal harm, whether appropriately classified as bullying or not.

QUESTIONS FOR REFLECTION

Does your school policy differentiate between bullying and other forms of interpersonal harm? Is such a differentiation necessary in your view?

3

CAN SOMEONE BE AN UNINTENTIONAL BULLY?

Justin W. Patchin

As the first two chapters suggest, defining bullying can be a tricky thing. And technology just adds another complicated layer to the whole situation. I mean, we know it when we see it, and at the extreme end, it's easy to identify: repeated threats, multiple humiliating posts, and numerous hurtful texts most likely qualify. But what about that mildly inappropriate joke directed at no one in particular? Or the post that reads, "I'm going to kill you. jk. lol"? Everyone seems to have a slightly different perspective when it comes to whether or not to categorize a particular experience as bullying.

BULLYING DEFINED

As referenced in the previous chapter, most definitions of bullying include an element of deliberateness or *intent*. Scandinavian researcher Dan Olweus, who is arguably most responsible for the current academic interest in the topic, defines bullying as "aggressive behavior that is intentional and that involves an imbalance of power. Most often, it is repeated over time."[9] The Minnesota

Department of Education states that "definitions of bullying vary, but most agree that bullying includes the intent to harm, repetition, and a power imbalance between the student targeted and the student who bullies."[10] Finally, StopBullying.gov defines bullying as "unwanted, aggressive behavior among school aged children that involves a real or perceived power imbalance." While this definition doesn't explicitly include intent, one could interpret "aggressive" to mean that the behavior in question was not unintentional.

In addition, many state bullying laws refer to intentional behaviors. Delaware law characterizes bullying as an "intentional written, electronic, verbal or physical act."[11] Louisiana defines cyberbullying as "the transmission of any electronic textual, visual, written, or oral communication with the malicious and willful intent to coerce, abuse, torment, or intimidate a person."[12] Indeed, intent is a fundamental component of criminal law generally. In order to hold someone criminally responsible, we must establish not only that the person engaged in a wrongful act, but also that he or she did so with *mens rea*—that is, a guilty mind. When it comes to law, however, there are always exceptions, and we furthermore believe that the vast majority of bullying incidents can and should be handled outside of the formal law. The point is that most academic and legal definitions of bullying include intent. But does that mean the criterion is necessary?

ACCIDENTAL BULLYING

Parenting advocate Sue Scheff wrote about "accidental" bullying and cyberbullying in an article for *The Huffington Post*.[13] She described incidents where teens say things to others, usually online, that aren't intended to be hurtful, but are experienced as such: "Even though it wasn't your objective, your words can be taken out of context by others when they're read and regurgitated, amplifying your digital footprint." This can happen offline as well, of course, but technology certainly does more easily obscure actual intent. Many of us know from personal experience that online interactions often lead to more frequent misunderstandings as communication occurs without important facial expressions, vocal intonations, or other interpretive behavioral cues that provide color and context to what is conveyed.

Scheff credits Internet safety educator Katie Greer for first alerting her to these types of behaviors. For Scheff's article, Greer explained accidental bullying in this way: "Oftentimes, kids described trying to be nice or positive to one friend or cause via various social networking sites, and unintentionally hurting someone's feelings, or leaving someone out in the process."[14] I agree that it is common for teens to say things to classmates or even to their best friends without malice or intent to cause harm, but for the comments even so to be misinterpreted or otherwise result in harm. But is this bullying?

The concept of an accidental bully is not new. Internet lawyer Parry Aftab has included the "inadvertent cyberbully" in her taxonomy since at least 2006: "They do it for the fun of it. They may also do it to one of their friends, joking around. But their friend may not recognize that it is another friend or make [sic] take it seriously."[15] According to Aftab, inad-

> It is common for teens to say things to classmates or even to their best friends without malice or intent to cause harm, but for the comments even so to be misinterpreted or otherwise result in harm. But is this bullying?

vertent cyberbullies "don't lash out intentionally,"[16] which is curious because she defines cyberbullying as "when minors use technology as a weapon to *intentionally* target and hurt another minor."[17] Like Greer, Aftab describes a situation where teens do or say something to be funny or even helpful, but it is misinterpreted or, for one reason or another, results in hurt feelings.

Greer offers an example in which the friends of a teen girl set up an online profile where people are asked to comment on or vote for the prettiest girl among four shown. The idea is to show their friend that she is very pretty. The profile creators stuff the virtual ballot box so that their friend emerges victorious, not realizing that by doing so the other three girls involved in the vote have had their feelings hurt (because, after all, they aren't the prettiest). Were the less-pretty girls in this example bullied? If the teens who created the site genuinely and honestly did not do so to cause harm to the girls who did not win, then I do not believe it is accurate to classify the incident as bullying.

Of course, the key to this is determining intent. It is possible that the girls responsible in Greer's example could have intended all along to take particular classmates down a notch by setting it up so they would emerge as losers. Or they may have rigged the vote in a way that one specific girl received significantly fewer votes than all of the rest, thereby securing her spot as the "least pretty." It would be correct to classify those cases as bullying, though definitely not accidental. But if the girls are sincere and authentic in stating that they really didn't mean to cause harm to those who were not voted the prettiest, then it isn't bullying. It should not be ignored, however, and the girls responsible should be informed about the unintended consequences of their actions so that they will refrain from similar behaviors in the future. Hopefully, that will be the end of the issue. If not, then subsequent intervention will be necessary.

CONTEXT IS IMPORTANT

Because it is impossible to know *for certain* what was going on in the mind of a teen when he or she behaved in a particular way, it is important to gather as much information as possible with which to determine whether the behavior in question could have been intentional. For example, is this the first time the particular student has been accused of bullying? Have there been behavioral problems with the student in the past? Were the students involved previously friends? Was there a falling-out? Did anyone else (other students or staff) notice previous problems between the students?

Of course, we need to keep in mind that just because a teen has never misbehaved in the past doesn't mean he or she didn't do so deliberately this time. And former friends often mistreat each other, especially if there was a recent issue that led to the breakup. The problematic behavior itself is only one piece of the puzzle. The more information you are able to gather about the nature of the relationships among all involved, the easier it will be to figure out what happened and why.

WHY IT MATTERS

For years, I deliberately remained on the sidelines when it came to debates like this. For me, whether some behavior was bullying or not really didn't matter. I advocated for identifying and focusing on the specific problematic behavior and addressing it for what it was. Unfortunately, this is no longer an option as some states have passed laws that mandate specific actions when it comes to behaviors defined as bullying.

Recall from Chapter 2 that New Jersey law requires principals to investigate every incident of bullying within one school day, and complete a formal report within ten days that must be submitted to the superintendent within two days of completion. In Georgia, students who are found to have bullied others for a third time are mandated to an alternative school. Furthermore, labeling a particular behavior as bullying can inflame a situation—especially if the label is being misapplied. So for the sake of administrator workload and student disciplinary actions, it has become imperative to clearly articulate what is meant by bullying.

I don't expect to resolve this decades-long definitional debate here, but I do hope to encourage researchers, policy makers, legislators, educators, and others who are charged with putting students in particular categories (e.g., "the bully") to think carefully about the criteria they use to make these decisions. Defining a person's behavior as bullying, or labeling someone "a bully," can set that person on a particular trajectory, and we best not do it capriciously or haphazardly.

QUESTIONS FOR REFLECTION

Do you feel intent is a necessary element to include in definitions of bullying? Can you think of an example where someone is genuinely "bullying" another unintentionally?

4

The Case for Including Intent in a Definition of Bullying

Justin W. Patchin

I recently presented at the International Bullying Prevention Association's annual conference. This was the second time that I participated in this event, and both experiences were enjoyable and educational. The attendees are generally very interested in the work that we are doing at the Cyberbullying Research Center, and the other presenters are uniformly among the best in the business.

The conversations that occur between the formal presentations are just as enlightening and thought provoking as anything within the scheduled sessions. Talking with attendees and other speakers sparks insights about issues we are working on and allows us to view our research and writing from the perspective of informed others. It was a couple of these conversations that ignited my interest in writing more about how we define bullying.

Right before my first presentation, I got to talking with author Stan Davis about how bullying is defined and specifically whether intent was a necessary component.[18] As discussed in Chapter 3, most definitions include this element, and ours is no different. Stan suggested that whether a behavior was deliberate or not is irrelevant. If it was hurtful, or if the person doing it should have known that it could have resulted in harm to another, then it was bullying. His position was supported by Elizabeth Englander, another researcher at the conference whose work I very much respect.[19] She added that the problem with including intent as a defining criterion is that it requires teachers in the classroom to get into the heads of students to try to figure out what they were thinking when they did what they did. This is a fair point, though one easy way to determine intent is to see if the behavior was repeated after some initial intervention. If the student is made aware that his or her behavior is causing harm to another (by either the target, a bystander, or someone else), yet he or she continues to behave in the same way, then it's clearly intentional.

After my presentation, Lori Ernsperger, another speaker who attended my session, came up to me to also discuss whether intent was really a necessary component of bullying.[20] Ernsperger and I chatted briefly about our respective positions on this issue, but because others were waiting to speak with me, we weren't able to dig into the details enough to clearly explain where we were coming from. I don't think that Stan, Elizabeth, and Lori collectively conspired to critique this component of my presentation, so I did feel the need to consider this question further.

That's why I was happy to receive an e-mail from Lori shortly after the conference with additional information about why she felt it was imperative that we adjust our definition by removing the element of intent. She was particularly concerned with the implications of requiring intent to define something as bullying when it came to behaviors targeting students with disabilities. "Disability harassment," she argued, "does not consider the intentionality of the bully, only if it is 'unwelcome conduct.' When the term 'willful' is used for defining bullying, it requires schools to have separate policies and definitions for students within protected classes."

She presented me with a hypothetical incident to consider:

A 16-year-old high school tennis player has a genetic disorder and diabetes. His teammates have been harassing him about going to the nurse's office and requiring more snack breaks during practice. This goes on for a year. Coaching staff have observed this, but as required by law (the Family Educational Rights and Privacy Act, or FERPA), most school personnel do not know he is a child with a disability. After repeated teasing, he stops going to the nurse and eventually drops out of tennis. This is a clear violation of his civil rights, but the school said it was not "intentional" on the part of the other students ("they were good kids from good homes and did not mean it"), and the personnel did not see this as willful behavior. But it does not matter. It was unwelcome conduct that changed this student's educational experience. All school personnel should observe and intervene regardless of the intentionality.

First of all, regardless of intent, I agree wholeheartedly with the final sentence in her vignette. School personnel should intervene whether the behavior is defined as bullying or not. One thing is clear: the tennis players were being mean to their teammate, and that should be addressed. But if the students involved in harassing the tennis player for a whole year genuinely didn't realize that what they were doing was harming the target, then it wasn't bullying. If the players were made aware that their comments were hurtful, especially by an authority figure like the coach or a school administrator, yet they continued to make them, then that would be evidence of intent. Or, perhaps, if a reasonable person would have known that the behaviors were causing harm, then it could be considered intentional and be accurately categorized as bullying. As I wrote about in Chapter 1, best friends can say things to each other that appear to be mean or that can unintentionally make each other upset. But are these things really bullying?

> Best friends can say things to each other that appear to be mean or that can unintentionally make each other upset. But are these things really bullying?

As a comparable example, maybe I say something to someone on a repeated basis, just thinking I am being funny, and that person completely ignores or even laughs along with what I am saying. But it turns out that the person is actually very hurt by my comments. Yet he never expresses that to me (nor does anyone else). What I am saying may be mean or rude, but it isn't bullying. Should it be addressed? Of course. Should it stop? Absolutely. If we were students at the same school, it would be completely appropriate for a teacher or counselor or whomever to make me aware of the harm that I am causing. At that point, I should definitely apologize and not do it again. If I do repeat it, then that clearly demonstrates willfulness because I was informed of the hurtful nature of what I was saying, but still continued. And that would be bullying.

Lori insisted that the "unwelcome conduct" standard is really what matters. If something is unwelcome, then it is bullying. I don't think it is that simple. What if I bump into someone in the hallway? Or spill my hot tea on someone's lap? What if I crash into another vehicle when its driver is stopped at a stoplight? These are all clear examples of unwelcome conduct, are they not? Would it be accurate to classify these as bullying—even if they were isolated events and completely accidental? Plus, in order for any of these behaviors to be considered "harassment" in a technical or legal sense, one would have to prove that they were done *because of* a person's status (based on race, class, gender, disability, etc.). Harassment is different from bullying. Some bullying behaviors could accurately be classified as harassment, and some harassment could be bullying. But the overlap is not 100%. For example, harassment (again, as formally defined) is always based on a protected status, whereas bullying is not. Harassment could be a singular incident (though often it is not), whereas bullying is always repetitive (or at least presents an imminent expectation of repetition). I still can't think of an example of a behavior where intent to cause harm is not present that would be accurately defined as bullying.

The bottom line is that we simply cannot call every harmful or hurtful or mean behavior between teens "bullying." That dilutes the problem and is confusing to everyone involved. Bullying is a specific and more serious form of interpersonal harm, and the term needs to be reserved for behaviors that are repeated and intentional.

QUESTIONS FOR REFLECTION

Stan Davis, Elizabeth Englander, and Lori Ernsperger are all experienced professionals when it comes to bullying. And yet we disagree about whether intent matters. What are your thoughts? Whom would you side with, and why?

ENDNOTES

1. Hazelden Foundation. (2016). *The Olweus Bullying Questionnaire.* Retrieved from http://www.violencepreventionworks.org/public/olweus_preparation.page#questionnaire

2. Bazelon, E. (2013, March 11). Defining bullying down. *The New York Times.* Retrieved from http://www.nytimes.com/2013/03/12/opinion/defining-bullying-down.html?_r=2; see also Bazelon, Emily. (2013). *Sticks and stones: Defeating the culture of bullying and rediscovering the power of character and empathy.* New York, NY: Random House.

3. I should point out that not everyone agrees with me on this point. Even though just about every reputable definition of *bullying* includes repetition, some would argue against it as a necessary element. Indeed, even New Jersey's Anti-Bullying Bill of Rights Act defines harassment, intimidation, or bullying as "any gesture, any written, verbal or physical act, or any electronic communication, whether it be *a single incident* or a series of incidents" (emphasis added). While I disagree with this legal definition of bullying, I recognize the state's desire to account for a variety of types of harmful behavior.

4. Hinduja, S., & Patchin, J. W. (2015). *Bullying beyond the schoolyard: Preventing and responding to cyberbullying* (2nd ed.). Thousand Oaks, CA: Corwin. Retrieved from http://www.cyberbullyingbook.com

5. Anti-Bullying Bill of Rights Statute, § 18A:37-13 et seq. [last updated in 2015]. Retrieved from http://lis.njleg.state.nj.us/cgi-bin/om_isapi.dll?clientID=252213&Depth=4&TD=WRAP&advquery=%2218A%3a37-13%22&headingswithhit

s=on&infobase=statutes.nfo&rank=&record={85FB}&softpage=Doc_Frame_
Pg42&wordsaroundhits=2&x=31&y=11&zz=

6. Walker, M. (2013, November 14). Is it bullying or drama? *The Huffington Post*. Retrieved from http://www.huffingtonpost.com/2013/11/13/bullying-or-drama_n_4268218.html; Wolak, J., Mitchell, K. J., & Finkelhor, D. (2007). Does online harassment constitute bullying? An exploration of online harassment by known peers and online-only contacts. *Journal of Adolescent Health*, *41*, S51–S58. Retrieved from http://www.unh.edu/ccrc/pdf/CV172.pdf

7. Ali, R. (2010, October 26). Dear colleague [Letter]. U.S. Department of Education, Office of Civil Rights. Retrieved from http://www2.ed.gov/about/offices/list/ocr/letters/colleague-201010.pdf

8. boyd, d., & Marwick, A. (2011, September 22). Bullying as true drama. *The New York Times*. Retrieved from http://www.nytimes.com/2011/09/23/opinion/why-cyberbullying-rhetoric-misses-the-mark.html; see also boyd, (2014). *It's complicated: The social lives of networked teens*. New Haven, CT: Yale University Press.

9. Hazelden Foundation. (2016). *Bullying is a serious issue*. Retrieved from http://www.violencepreventionworks.org/public/bullying.page; see also Olweus, D. (1993). *Bullying at school: What we know and what we can do*. Cambridge, MA: Blackwell.

10. Minnesota Department of Education. (2015). *Bullying and cyber-bullying*. Retrieved from http://education.state.mn.us/MDE/StuSuc/SafeSch/BullyiCyberBullyPrev/index.html

11. State of Delaware. (n.d.). Title 14: Education: Free Public Schools. Chapter 41. General Regulatory Provisions, § 4112D School Bullying Prevention. Retrieved from http://delcode.delaware.gov/title14/c041/index.shtml#4112D

12. Louisiana State Legislature. (n.d.). RS 14 § 40.7. Cyberbullying. Retrieved from http://legis.la.gov/Legis/law.aspx?d=725180

13. Scheff, S. (2013, October, 30). Accidental bullying and cyberbullying. *The Huffington Post*. Retrieved from http://www.huffingtonpost.com/sue-scheff/accidental-bullying-and-c_b_3843092.html?utm_hp_ref=tw

14. Ibid.

15. Aftab, P. (n.d.). Offsite Internet activities and schools: What methods work with the different kinds of cyberbullies? *STOP Cyberbullying*. Retrieved from http://www.stopcyberbullying.org/educators/howdoyouhandleacyberbully.html

16. Ibid.

17. Aftab, P. (2006–2011). A parent's guide to cyberbullying [emphasis added]. *Wired Safety*. Retrieved from https://www.wiredsafety.org/toolkitmedia/files/file/Parent_s_Articles/A_Parent_s_Guide_to_Cyberbullying_-_Extended.pdf

18. Stan Davis (2003) is the author of *Schools where everyone belongs: Practical strategies for reducing bullying*. Wayne, ME: Stop Bullying Now.

19. See, for example, Englander, E. (2013). *Bullying and cyberbullying: What every educator needs to know*. Cambridge, MA: Harvard Education Press.

20. Lori Ernsperger (2016) is the author of *recognize, respond, report: Preventing and addressing bullying of students with special needs*. Baltimore, MD: Brookes.

PART II

BULLYING BY THE NUMBERS

What We Know

5

160,000 Students Stay Home From School Every Day Because of Bullying?

Justin W. Patchin

At the Cyberbullying Research Center, we strive to approach the issue of teen technology use and misuse from a data-informed perspective. Just to be clear, *data* doesn't just mean bar charts. Since 2002, we have formally surveyed over 15,000 middle and high school students, so yes, we have a lot of bar charts. But we have also spoken to thousands of teens in schools all around the United States (and abroad). We get e-mails and phone calls daily from teens, parents, educators, and others who care about the online behaviors of young people. We have done focused interviews with small groups of students. We also review research articles written by other scholars (both published and unpublished).[1] All of these are valuable sources of data. Taken together, they can help us develop a more comprehensive understanding of what is really going on.

Some data sources are definitely better than others, and we must take into consideration the quality of the source and the sophistication of the methodology when interpreting results. Randomly selecting participants from a known group (or *sample*) is much better, for example, than arbitrarily selecting people who happen to be at a particular place and time.

To illustrate, I was recently at a school where a teacher told me that *every* student at her school had either seen or engaged in sexting. When pressed, she admitted that this was not a scientific survey, just a questioning of a few of the students coming out of the cafeteria one day. She extrapolated that to conclude that "everyone" at her school was in some way involved in sexting. Of course, this is ridiculous. I haven't seen a sexting study report prevalence rates higher than 31% for receiving a "sext," and most studies put the rate in the teens.[2] In fact, the Crimes Against Children Research Center recently reported that only 7.1% of students between the ages of 10 and 17 had received a sext (and this was a nationally representative survey—about as good as you can get methodologically).[3]

> Misinformation tends to lead to knee-jerk, emotionally driven responses, which is the last thing we need when attempting to deal with such a complex and enduring problem.

So, whenever I find a particular statistic cited, I first attempt to uncover the original source and then review the methodology. What was the sample? (For more on this, see Chapter 7.) How were participants selected to be in that sample? What specific questions were asked? Take, once again, the issue of sexting. How exactly is sexting defined? If you ask teens whether they have *ever* seen a nude image of another person, the number who say yes will likely be very high (if they are being truthful). If you ask them, on the other hand, if they have seen a nude image of another student from their school *in the last 30 days*, the number will be much lower. This is the question that we asked in our research, but even it can be misinterpreted.

This brings me to the original point of this chapter. I have seen too many times to count the statistic that over 160,000 students stay home every school day due to bullying. This statistic has popped up on numerous websites that appear to be legitimate reporters of bullying research. Interestingly, I see it most commonly cited in news reports and governmental reports. I even found it in a *New York Times* article from over 20 years ago.[4] I've also seen it twice recently in summaries for bullying prevention programs being offered by experts.

Do a Google search for that statistic, and you will see it pop up thousands of times. But where did it come from? It has been attributed to many different sources. Most commonly, it is credited to the Centers for Disease Control and Prevention (CDC). At least one CDC report cites a book written in 1998

(*Real Boys: Rescuing Our Sons From the Myths of Boyhood* by William Pollack).[5] That book attributes the statistic to the National Association of School Psychologists, but doesn't provide a citation to a specific study or source. Again, where did it come from? I have put the question to some of the brightest minds in the area of bullying prevention and research, and nobody knows for sure.

There is no question that too many students stay home from school every day because of fear of bullying. However, the exact number is difficult to really know. Frankly, *it could be much higher than 160,000*. But it does our field a disservice to report statistics without being able to substantiate them. Bullying *is* a serious problem that warrants our attention. But that case can be made using reliable and valid statistics, not hyperbole. Misinformation tends to lead to knee-jerk, emotionally driven responses, which is the last thing we need when attempting to deal with such a complex and enduring problem.

QUESTIONS FOR REFLECTION

Why is it important to use valid data when reporting statistics on bullying? What are some of the consequences of not using good data? Are you collecting useful data about the behaviors of your students?

6

CYBERBULLYING

Neither an Epidemic nor a Rarity

Justin W. Patchin

If you pay attention to the news reports of cyberbullying incidents (as we do), you probably think that these inappropriate online behaviors are happening at "epidemic" levels (whatever that really even means). When we first started studying cyberbullying in 2002, we would literally print out any news article we saw that talked about cyberbullying—because it happened (or at least was reported) so infrequently. Now, it seems, cyberbullying occurs (and is reported) at an almost constant rate. To test this theory, set up a Google Alert with the keyword "cyberbullying" and see how many articles come through every day. Your in-box will be inundated.

In contrast to this perspective, the argument has been advanced that cyberbullying is not occurring at levels that require our significant attention. Specifically, Professor Dan Olweus, who has done more to advance the scholarship of school bullying than anyone else in the world, argued in 2012 that "cyberbullying is a basically low-frequent phenomenon and that there has not occurred a marked increase in the prevalence rates of cyberbullying over the past five or six years."[6] We agree with Professor Olweus on most issues but believe that the nature and extent of cyberbullying does warrant independent empirical, legal, and educational attention. We were honored to be invited to write a commentary on Professor Olweus's remarks.[7]

So how much cyberbullying is really occurring? Is it an epidemic or a rarity? Well, the answer, as you might guess, is somewhere in between. To be sure, we have written quite a bit about this question. In *Cyberbullying Prevention and Response: Expert Perspectives*, we reviewed all of the empirical research that had been published as of 2011 and found that across 35 refereed articles, from 5.5% to 72% of students had been cyberbullied and from 6% to 30% of students had admitted to cyberbullying others.[8] In the most recent edition of *Bullying Beyond the Schoolyard: Preventing and Responding to Cyberbullying*, we updated this analysis to include 74 peer-reviewed articles, and the rates didn't change all that much (from 2.3% to 72% for being victimized and from 1.2% to 44.1% for offending).[9]

As mentioned in Chapter 5, we've surveyed over 15,000 middle and high school students from a variety of schools across the United States. Our first studies were online convenience samples, intended only to gather early information about an emerging problem. Our last nine studies, however, were all conducted among random samples of known student populations in schools. Across those samples, the percentage of students who reported being the victim of cyberbullying ranged from 18.8% to 34.6% (average 26.3%). Similarly, 11.5% to 19.4% of students admitted to cyberbullying others at some point in their lifetimes (average 16.2%).[10]

> How much cyberbullying is really occurring? Is it an epidemic or a rarity? Well, the answer, as you might guess, is somewhere in between.

Even though we have done 11 different surveys since 2002, we aren't able to look at the data in a way that identifies trends because most of our research involved different school populations. Lisa Jones, Kimberly J. Mitchell, and David Finkelhor from the Crimes Against Children Research Center at the University of New Hampshire collected data from students across the United States in 2000, 2005, and 2010 and saw a modest but steady increase in cyberbullying (from 6% in 2000 to 11% in 2010).[11] Their numbers are lower than ours because of the different way they conducted their research, but since they looked at cyberbullying the same way in three different national studies, we can use the results to estimate that cyberbullying in general seems to be increasing.

The School Crime Supplement to the National Crime Victimization Survey, which utilizes a representative sample of students in the United States, added a handful of cyberbullying questions in 2009, and those data showed that 6% reported being bullied "by electronic means anywhere."[12] In 2011, that number increased to 9% though it decreased to 6.9% in 2013 (the most recent data available).[13] So where does this leave us? Professor Olweus is right that cyberbullying isn't some new phenomenon that is completely distinct from the bullying that has been perpetrated by and toward teens for generations. But it is occurring at levels that demand our attention. We know that most cyberbullying is connected to offline relationships and that most teens who cyberbully also bully at school (for more on this, see Chapter 10). Cyberbullying is neither an epidemic nor a rarity. But it is something that everyone has a responsibility to work toward ending.

QUESTIONS FOR REFLECTION

Why do you think the numbers reported in the research vary so significantly? How do the rates reported in national research compare to the experiences of students in your school?

7

Small Samples Don't Speak "Truth"

Justin W. Patchin

Our primary mission at the Cyberbullying Research Center is to translate the research we and others do into something that is meaningful and interpretable to teens, parents, educators, and others dedicated to preventing and responding more effectively to cyberbullying. When we launched our website, cyberbullying.org, in 2005, there wasn't much research being done, so it was easy to keep up. These days, however, many scholars are putting cyberbullying experiences under the microscope, which is a very good thing. It is important to recognize, though, that not all studies are created equal. In this chapter, I'd like to discuss one particular problem: small sample sizes. And, to be more specific, I am most concerned with the way some media reports make definitive, sweeping generalizations from these studies.

For illustrative purposes, I'd like to highlight two recently published articles that gained some measure of attention by the media. I think they attracted this interest, in part, because their findings speak to the conventional wisdom regarding cyberbullying (that is, that traditional bullying is worse than cyberbullying, and that people don't really want to intervene when they see it happen). I'm all for using data to help validate or refute commonly held beliefs about cyberbullying.[14] Many of the media reports about these articles, however, make broad, seemingly conclusive generalized statements based on the perspectives or experiences of a very small group of students.

TRADITIONAL BULLYING IS MORE HARMFUL THAN CYBERBULLYING

The first article was written by Emma-Kate Corby and five of her Australian colleagues.[15] The authors analyzed responses from 156 middle and high school students (114 female, 42 male) who were victims of both traditional bullying and cyberbullying for the primary purpose of determining which the students themselves believed to be worse. A typical headline about this study stated that "Cyber bullying [Is] Not as Concerning as Face-to-Face for Kids."[16] Is this true?

> Many media reports make broad, seemingly conclusive generalized statements based on the perspectives or experiences of a very small group of students.

According to the results, of the students who had experienced both forms of bullying, 59% said that the face-to-face form was worse while 15% said the cyberbullying was worse (26% said it was about the same). So, at least among the majority of students in this particular sample, the face-to-face form of bullying was worse. Interestingly, *we* hear quite often from teens that the online forms of bullying they experience are worse for them than the at-school forms they have to endure. Which "sample" is more reflective of the experiences of most youth: theirs or ours?

I personally believe that the answer to the question of "which is worse" varies significantly by student and by experience. A blanket statement that "*all* cyberbullying is less impactful for *all* students than *all* forms of face-to-face bullying" is too far-reaching of a conclusion to draw. While media reports might suggest that, the authors of the article certainly did not imply this. Some teens *are* significantly impacted by online experiences, and others are not. It is very person specific.

I should point out that I know a few of the authors of this article and genuinely respect their work. As such, I cannot dismiss the findings outright. But I don't think they would generalize their results as broadly as some media reports have done (even if their findings do get supported by subsequent research).

FEW STUDENTS WILLING TO STEP UP WHEN THEY WITNESS CYBERBULLYING

A second article, written by Kelly Dillon and Brad Bushman (both from the School of Communication at Ohio State), was published in 2015.[17] This study sought to determine if people would be willing to directly intervene if they witnessed mistreatment in an online chat room. The sample comprised 221 university students (154 female, 67 male). It is unclear how students were selected to participate in the study or if they were representative of the population from which they were drawn (presumably, Ohio State students).

The researchers set up a scenario where students were invited to evaluate a chat support platform for online surveys. Once in the chat room, a confederate (one of the researchers) began mistreating a third party in the room. Only 10% of participants who noticed the behavior intervened directly (by messaging the target or aggressor, or by contacting the lead researcher). In addition, about two-thirds of the participants intervened indirectly by rating the chat environment (or the chat monitor) poorly on an exit evaluation. I'm not sure how this latter behavior represents an "intervention," but I suppose it is meant to be a proxy for some kind of online reporting mechanism.

Most of the media headlines that reported on this study focused on the finding that few students directly intervened. But also consider this headline from *The Inquisitr*: "Online Trolls, Cyber-Bullying Succeeds Because No One Intervenes or Stands-Up Against the Bullies, Prove Scientists."[18] I am particularly perturbed by the use of "No One Intervenes" and "Prove Scientists." Nothing was "proven" in this study, and it is factually incorrect to say that "no one" intervened. But that was the headline.

We saw similar conclusions drawn from a video that went viral in 2014 that seemingly showed university students unwilling to intervene when they saw someone being roughed up right before their eyes.[19] As with research published in academic journals, we need to ask ourselves if the persons depicted in the video are representative of the general population. That is, we need to carefully consider whether the behaviors featured in the clip (and, by extension, in the previous two studies) are typical of what *most* people would do. The goal of research is to identify that which is not unique or random, but rather that which occurs with some regularity and consistency. Larger samples help to reduce the likelihood that what is observed is extraordinary.

WHAT CAN WE LEARN?

The important take-home message from these studies is that more research is necessary. Even though it may well turn out that the results from these studies are valid, it is still unwise to draw concrete conclusions from any single study, especially one that involves just a couple hundred respondents. Small samples are fine for exploratory purposes: to pilot an untested measure or explore a new research question. They should be used to guide more comprehensive investigations in the future, not to create policy or generate page-clicks with disingenuous headlines.

We try to base what few definitive conclusions can be drawn on the weight of prevailing research, rather than just one study. For example, when we say that about one out of every four or five students has experienced cyberbullying in his or her lifetime, we are basing that on the 11 surveys we have done (which have included more than 15,000 respondents), as well as our painstaking review of 74 articles published in peer-reviewed journals since 2002 (which have included nearly 150,000 respondents).[20]

> It is still unwise to draw concrete conclusions from any single study, especially one that involves just a couple hundred respondents.

Determining whether a sample is "small" depends more on the size of the population it is intended to represent than the raw number of people surveyed. If a school has 60,000 university students, for instance, and you only study 200 of them, you are examining just one-third of one percent of the population (0.3%). Should we expect that those 200 are substantially similar (based on perceptions and experiences) to all 60,000? A carefully selected (usually randomly chosen) sample of sufficient size (such as from 5% to 10%) *would* allow us to draw some conclusions without having to survey every single person. But if I poll the first 20 students who walk into my building, it is unlikely that their beliefs and behaviors are representative of my university population of 11,000.

Don't get me wrong—our samples aren't perfect either. Much social science research is plagued with problems, some of which are unavoidable. We all make concessions when asking certain questions to certain people at certain times. Also, gaining access to a large and representative sample of students is very difficult. In order to really make progress in growing our knowledge base related to cyberbullying, though, it is critical for researchers to do the best they can while acknowledging any limitations. And journalists have an obligation to report findings accurately and responsibly, without making grandiose claims that often fail to capture the true picture of what is going on.

QUESTIONS FOR REFLECTION

Why is it important to have a relatively large sample when conducting studies on bullying? Why do you think the media overemphasizes the results of particular studies?

8

Ban School, Open Facebook

Justin W. Patchin

There is much consternation among parents and educators alike about the perceived criminogenic nature of social media websites and apps. Despite some evidence that its popularity among some teens is beginning to wane, Facebook is still the most prominent figure in this space.[21] As such, it tends to receive the brunt of the blows, with fervent calls from well-meaning adults to ban teen access to the site and others like it. Take one principal's plea to parents back in 2010: "There is absolutely, positively no reason for any middle school student to be a part of a social networking site! None."[22] To be sure, there are plenty of good reasons to limit time on social media, especially for younger Internet users. But when it comes to bullying behaviors specifically, the evidence is clear that school is a much more "dangerous" place to hang out than Facebook.

BULLYING VS. CYBERBULLYING

At its core, bullying in all its forms involves deliberate and repeated hurtful actions directed toward another who can't easily defend him- or herself (see Chapter 2). While technology has created additional avenues and opportunities for this to occur, it really hasn't created a whole new class of youth who bully others *only* from afar. In general, those who bully online also bully at school (for more on this, see Chapter 10).

Moreover, just about *every study* that has included measures of both bullying at school and bullying online has shown that the former still occurs more frequently. I realize the counterintuitiveness of this statement, but the consistency of this discrepancy is compelling. For example, the National Crime Victimization Survey's biennially conducted survey of students (the School Crime Supplement) showed that of primary and secondary students, 21.8% were bullied at school while 6.7% were bullied online in 2013 (the most recent data available).

> In general, those who bully online also bully at school.

Similarly, across the 11 studies we have conducted, the prevalence rates for cyberbullying have been significantly less than those for traditional school bullying. In our 2010 study involving 4,400 middle and high school students, 26% reported that they had been recently bullied at school while 8% said that they had been recently bullied online (4% on Facebook specifically). In February 2015, we surveyed 450 middle schoolers in a school in the Midwest and found that 33% had been bullied at school, and 7% on Facebook, in the previous 30 days.

To be fair, some evidence shows that the gap may be narrowing. Bullying at school has been steady or declining in recent years while cyberbullying may be creeping up, but certainly not at the pace that most perceive.[23]

One of the challenges in trying to make sense of all of the data on different forms of bullying is that survey questions are often phrased problematically. If you ask someone—especially a teen—if he or she has been bullied, unless instructed otherwise, he or she is going to report *any* experience with bullying, irrespective of *where* it happened. Asking, for instance, if anyone has spread rumors or repeatedly said mean or hurtful things to someone doesn't specify a particular location, so we don't know exactly where it happened. As a result, it is quite possible that some bullying experiences that are interpreted as having occurred at school may have happened online (or, even more likely, in both environments).

There is no doubt that we hear about more high-profile cases of cyberbullying on the nightly news, which gives the illusion that it is the more prevalent problem. And, with the rapid expansion of technology in the hands of teenagers over the last decade or so, it isn't unreasonable to presume a precipitous increase in technology-related problematic behaviors. But it's just not true.

FOCUS ON CYBERBULLYING STILL NECESSARY

Please don't misunderstand—I am certainly not suggesting that we should ignore cyberbullying. It's still a significant problem that affects a meaningful number of teens.[24] In the summer of 2015, we scrutinized all of the peer-reviewed academic journal articles we could find that included cyberbullying prevalence rates. Across the 122 articles we examined that included victimization data, on average, about 21% of the teens surveyed said they had been cyberbullied. While the numbers published in these articles vary widely (from less than 1% to a high of 92%), one thing is certain: cyberbullying is happening, and it doesn't have to.

We need to condemn bullying in all its forms. Whether it happens online or at school—on Facebook or on the bus—efforts need to be taken to prevent and appropriately respond to all instances of serious and repetitive mistreatment. But, limiting access to Facebook for the purposes of preventing cyberbullying is akin to restricting access to school with the goal of preventing face-to-face bullying. Just as someone could spread rumors about another person at school without the target being there, the same is true about online environments. Instead, adults need to teach youth to use technology responsibly and regularly check in with them to ensure that they are doing so. We must also empower teens themselves to be a solution to the bullying problem by equipping them with tools that they can utilize should they experience it or see it happening at school or online. Working together, teens and adults can be a formidable force to counter cruelty, no matter what it looks like or where it happens.

> Adults need to teach youth to use technology responsibly and regularly check in with them to ensure that they are doing so.

QUESTIONS FOR REFLECTION

Does bullying happen more at school or online in your community? On what do you base this answer? Do you think banning access to social media websites and apps would prevent bullying?

9

DOES BULLYING "CAUSE" SUICIDE?

Justin W. Patchin

The title of Deborah Temkin's 2013 *Huffington Post* article is a simple request: "Stop Saying Bullying Causes Suicide."[25] Temkin is a senior research scientist for Child Trends who formerly helped to coordinate anti-bullying efforts for the U.S. Department of Education and the Obama administration. Her plea is understandable and justified. We too cringe when we read the ubiquitous headlines espousing the conventional wisdom proclaiming that bullying causes suicide. But what does the research actually say about the relationship between bullying and suicide?

Temkin rightly points to a handful of studies showing some truth to the assertion that bullying plays a role in some suicides.[26] But it is also true that most teens involved in bullying do not die by suicide.[27] Most people who have spent some time exploring the connection understand that—like any association in the social sciences—it is often much more complicated than simply X causes Y. There are a number of known factors related to suicide that, combined with other situational or enduring life stressors (such as bullying), can predict risk. But even so, most people who experience these do not commit suicide.[28]

I think it is just as important to remember that, as inappropriate as it is to definitively assert that bullying causes suicide, it is perhaps equally incorrect to say that bullying does *not* cause suicide. The frank truth is that we really don't know. I'm not aware of any research that has tested the "bullying causes suicide" hypothesis and returned null findings. Most research that I am aware of, including the few samples where we include questions about suicidal ideology and attempts, shows a significant, though admittedly modest, relationship in the expected direction—namely, that experience with bullying is a factor in suicide, not the opposite.[29] Of course, other variables, like the risk factors noted above, play an important role.

One realization I have come to is that it is not helpful to tell members of a grieving family that bullying was not the cause of their child's death, when in their hearts they know it was. I am not going to stand in front of them and tell them that they are wrong. Here's what we do know: most young people who are bullied do not resort to suicide. Some do. Whether it's causal or correlational or part of a whole constellation of co-occurring challenges in the lives of certain youths, it simply does not change what we all are trying to do. We seek to inform the problem of teen suicide with data, and the empirical and anecdotal data that do exist (however limited) lend more credibility to a relationship than not. Please don't misread this as defending the media for often misrepresenting the nature of the problem, but we shouldn't overplay our hand either.

> Most young people who are bullied do not resort to suicide. Some do.

As such, I would offer an addendum to Temkin's *Huffington Post* appeal: Yes, people should "Stop Saying Bullying Causes Suicide."[30] But we also shouldn't say that it doesn't. The honest answer is that we really don't know a whole lot about why some teens who are bullied consider suicide whereas the vast majority do not. As in many cases, more research is necessary.

Of course, if you or a friend is contemplating suicide, please contact the National Suicide Prevention Lifeline at 1-800-273-TALK.

QUESTIONS FOR REFLECTION

Why do you think it is so difficult to determine the causes of teen suicide? Why do some teens consider or commit suicide after experiencing bullying but others do not? How can we better prevent teen suicide?

10

Most Who Bully Online Bully at School

Justin W. Patchin

Technology has given students immeasurable opportunities to communicate with friends and collaborate on schoolwork. Of course, it also allows those with ill intent to use technology to engage in antisocial behavior. One question that we have been exploring is the extent to which technology has created a whole new class of individuals who mistreat others. Think about it: If I want to be cruel to someone else, but perhaps don't feel comfortable or confident to do so at school, I may turn to the Internet. This may be because I am proficient using various social media environments, or because I need time to craft my ingenious hateful statement or execute my brilliant plan to humiliate someone else, or because I would get beaten up if I tried to do it in person, or because I would be more likely to get caught at school. There are many potential "benefits" to bullying from behind the screen of a device.

I was recently reviewing our 2010 data from over 4,400 middle and high school students whom we randomly selected from one large school district to explore this question. What I found was that very few students reported that they had cyberbullied others but had not bullied others at school. Specifically, 34% of the sample had bullied at school only, and 10% had bullied at school and online, but just 1.1% had bullied online only. So most of those who are doing the bullying online are also doing the bullying at school (90% of those who cyberbully also engage in school bullying). I checked the data from one of our more recent studies (a sample of about 600 middle school students collected in 2014) and found that of the less than 5% of students who had cyberbullied others in the previous 30 days, nearly 75% had also bullied at school.

So what does this mean for how we should respond to cyberbullying? First, some educators have argued that if the behavior does not happen at school, there is nothing that they can do. While this perspective is incorrect (see Chapter 35), our research shows that there is a high likelihood that a student who is involved in cyberbullying is also involved in bullying at school. Either way, educators should be involved in reasonably responding to all bullying, no matter where it happens, if those behaviors inhibit the ability of students to learn and feel safe at school.

> Educators should be involved in reasonably responding to all bullying, no matter where it happens, if those behaviors inhibit the ability of students to learn and feel safe at school.

Second, the causes of bullying are likely similar irrespective of the environment in which the bullying takes place. That is, whatever causes students to bully online will undoubtedly also cause them to bully in person. As much as technology has made it easier to connect with others at any time and from just about any place, the trigger or primary opportunity for bullying still appears to come at school. It will be interesting to see if this changes over time. Most people we speak to often assume that cyberbullying is occurring with more frequency than traditional schoolyard bullying. Maybe that is because most of what we hear about in the news involves cases of cyberbullying or because technology is so much more widespread among teens than ever before. The reality, however, is that most bullying is still happening at school (see Chapter 8).

These findings do raise some interesting follow-up questions for additional study. For example, are certain characteristics unique to the group of students who specialize in only one form of bullying? Are interventions that focus on reducing bullying generally also effective at reducing cyberbullying (or vice versa)? Do certain features of schools (or web environments) make them more or less inviting for different types of bullying? And how can we specifically support students who act out in interpersonal harm offline or online to determine what is prompting those behaviors?

QUESTIONS FOR REFLECTION

Why do you think students engage in bullying? Do you think the reasons are different when it comes to online bullying versus schoolyard bullying?

11

Cyberbullying Less Emotionally Impactful Than In-Person Bullying?

Justin W. Patchin

Researchers at the Crimes Against Children Research Center at the University of New Hampshire (UNH) published an article in the journal *Psychology of Violence* that explores the question of whether technology "amplifies" the harm for youth who are harassed.[31] Anecdotally, we have heard this to be the case from many youth over the years: that the bullying they experienced online was *as bad as*, and in some cases *much worse than*, the bullying that they experienced at school. Adolescent targets often reported feeling less equipped to stop cyberbullying, and indicated they faced more barriers when confiding in adults about these behaviors. Educators have policies and are trained to deal with the bullying that occurs on school grounds, but up until very recently, this wasn't the case for online bullying that occurred away from school. Moreover, sometimes the aggressors are anonymous, and the hurtful content is posted in a public place for all to see. So, in many ways, online bullying seems to have *the potential* to be much worse for some who experience it.

But one particular finding in the UNH article has called this conventional wisdom into question. Specifically, students who experienced cyberbullying by itself (with no accompanying in-person bullying) were less emotionally impacted than those who experienced face-to-face bullying. The media has interpreted this to mean that cyberbullying is not as bad as in-person bullying.[32] This is part of the story, but not the whole story.

> Online bullying has the potential to be much worse for some who experience it.

DIFFERENT METHODOLOGY

Kimberly Mitchell and her colleagues took a somewhat unique approach to studying youth harassment.[33] Instead of simply asking students to report whether they had been bullied (online or offline) and how many times they had experienced various forms of bullying during the previous year, the researchers drilled down on particular incidents and detailed questions about the bullying respondents had experienced in a singular incident. This is different from most other research in that the unit of analysis in this study is *the incident*, not the student. Mitchell and her colleagues interviewed 791 students, and 230 of them (29%) had been bullied at least once in the previous year. If students had been bullied more than once, researchers asked about the most recent and the most serious incident (focusing on a maximum of only two unique incidents). This led to 311 independent incidents of bullying (about a third of the students were bullied more than once). Of those incidents, 44% involved in-person bullying, 19% involved cyberbullying, and 38% involved both.

Those who were bullied both online and offline—*in the same incident*—were the most distressed by their experience: "Mixed incidents had the most emotional impact, possibly because they occurred across multiple environments and because perpetrators tended to be more socially connected to victims."[34] Indeed, if we review many of the high-profile incidents where teens took their own lives after experiencing cyberbullying, we see that in addition to the online bullying, the teens struggled with family and social problems, including being bullied at school.

As noted in the previous chapter, we find that youth who are bullied online are also very often bullied at school. For example, in our 2014 survey of about 650 middle school students from the northeastern United States, we found that 12.4% of students had been cyberbullied within the previous 30 days. Over 80% of those students were also bullied at school during the same time period. So it is very likely that students who are being bullied online are also being bullied at school. The UNH study doesn't necessarily account for these kinds of crossover experiences if the student views them as separate incidents.

OTHER INTERESTING FINDINGS

Also of note, even though most researchers define bullying in a way that requires repetition and a power differential, 12% of the students who said they were harassed in the UNH study reported that there was no power differential, and only 41% said it happened repeatedly. This, of course, calls into question our definitions of bullying.[35] Sameer and I published an article in the journal *Aggression and Violent Behavior* that discusses these issues in much more detail.[36] Mitchell and her colleagues have always used the term *peer harassment* instead of *bullying* because they recognize the important differences between the two types of behaviors.[37] So, to be precise, this is a study not of bullying, but of the broader experiences of peer harassment (see Chapter 2 for a discussion of some of the differences between harassment and bullying).

CONCLUSION

So, does technology amplify harm for youth? Even though most reports based on this article conclude that the answer to this question is no, that clearly does not follow directly from the results. For just about every emotional outcome explored (upset, embarrassed, worried, angry, sad, unsafe, lack of trust), the percentage of students who reported experiencing each outcome *increased* when technology was a factor in the harassment. For example, of the 136 incidents where students were harassed only in person, 13% resulted in embarrassment. Of the 117 incidents where students were harassed in person *and* online, 30% were embarrassed. Similarly, 22% of the in-person incidents, compared to 34% of the mixed incidents, left students worried. Also, 15% of students who experienced an in-person-only incident felt like they couldn't trust people, compared to 42% of the students who experienced harassment in person and online. Finally, the average total "emotional impact score" was 19.1 for in-person-only incidents, compared to 23.1 for mixed incidents.

So it sure seems like technology amplifies some of the emotional harm. And previous research has supported the anecdotal evidence discussed at the beginning of the chapter. Rina Bonanno and Shelley Hymel found that involvement in cyberbullying was associated with increased depression and suicidal ideation, even when controlling for experiences with traditional bullying.[38] As always, the reality is likely much more complicated than researchers (or especially the media) can succinctly summarize in a headline. As Campbell, Spears, Slee, Butler, and Kift found in a 2012 study,

> *although students who had been victimised by traditional bullying reported that they felt their bullying was harsher, crueler and had more impact on their lives than those students who had been cyber-bullied, the correlates of their mental health revealed that cyber victims reported significantly more social difficulties, higher anxiety levels and depression than traditional victims.*[39]

Focusing only on the singular finding that those who were "just" cyber-bullied felt less harmed than those who were bullied only in person misses a lot of important insights we can learn from this study. I don't believe that the takeaway message from the UNH study is that cyberbullying is not as bad as in-person bullying (even though that seems to be the focus in the media). It is just as accurate to conclude that "Technology Increases the Emotional Harms Associated With Bullying."

QUESTIONS FOR REFLECTION

Based on your experience working with youth who have been bullied, which form of bullying do you think impacts them more? Why is it important to determine whether bullying at school is worse for students than bullying online?

ENDNOTES

1 Patchin, J. W., & Hinduja, S. (2012). Cyberbullying: An update and synthesis of the research. In J. W. Patchin & S. Hinduja (Eds.), *Cyberbullying prevention and response: Expert perspectives* (pp. 13–36). New York, NY: Routledge.

2. Mitchell, K. J., Finkelhor, D., Jones, L. M., & Wolak, J. (2012). Prevalence and characteristics of youth sexting: A national study. *Pediatrics*, *129*, 13–20; Strassberg, D. S., McKinnon, R. K., Sustaíta, M. A., & Rullo, J. (2013). Sexting by high school students: An exploratory and descriptive study. *Archives of Sexual Behavior*, *42*, 15–21.

3. Mitchell, K. J., Finkelhor, D., Jones, L. M., & Wolak, J. (2012). Prevalence and characteristics of youth sexting: A national study. *Pediatrics*, *129*, 13–20.

4. Lee, F. R. (1993, April 4). Disrespect rules. *The New York Times*. Retrieved from http://www.nytimes.com/1993/04/04/education/disrespect-rules.html?src=pm

5. Centers for Disease Control and Prevention. (2011, May 3). *Understanding school violence fact sheet, 2010*. Retrieved from http://www.cdc.gov/ncipc/dvp/YVP/SV_Factsheet.pdf; for Pollack's book, see http://www.williampollack.com/real_boys_intro.html

6. Olweus, D. (2012). Cyberbullying: An overall phenomenon? *European Journal of Developmental Psychology, 9*, 520–538. doi:10.1080/17405629.2012.705086

7. For more information, see Hinduja, S., & Patchin, J. W. (2012). Cyberbullying: Neither an epidemic nor a rarity. *European Journal of Developmental Psychology, 9*, 539–543.

8. Patchin, J. W., & Hinduja, S. (2012). *Cyberbullying prevention and response: Expert perspectives*. New York, NY: Routledge.

9. Hinduja, S., & Patchin, J. W. (2015). *Bullying beyond the schoolyard: Preventing and responding to cyberbullying* (2nd ed.). Thousand Oaks, CA: Corwin.

10. For more information about our methodology, see cyberbullying.org/research.

11. Jones, L. M., Mitchell, K. J., & Finkelhor, D. (2013). Online harassment in context: Trends from three youth Internet safety surveys (2000, 2005, 2010). *Psychology of Violence, 3*, 53–69. Retrieved from http://psycnet.apa.org/journals/vio/3/1/53

12. DeVoe, J. F., & Hill, M. (2011). *Student victimization in U.S. schools: Results from the 2009 School Crime Supplement to the National Crime Victimization Survey*. Washington, DC: U.S. Government Printing Office, p. 11. Retrieved from http://nces.ed.gov/pubs2012/2012314.pdf

13. Institute of Education Sciences. (2013). *Student reports of bullying and cyber bullying: Results from the 2013 School Crime Supplement to the National Crime Victimization Survey*. Retrieved from http://nces.ed.gov/pubs2015/2015056.pdf

14. See, for example, Sabella, R. A., Patchin, J. W., & Hinduja, S. (2013). Cyberbullying myths and realities. *Computers in Human Behavior, 29*, 2703–2711.

15. Corby, E., Campbell, M., Spears, B., Slee, P., Butler, D., & Kift, S. (2015). Students' perceptions of their own victimization: A youth voice perspective. *Journal of School Violence*. Advance online publication. doi:10.1080/15388220.2014.996719

16. Branco, J. (2015, March 11). Cyber bullying not as concerning as face-to-face for kids: Study. *Brisbane Times*. Retrieved from http://www.brisbanetimes.com.au/queensland/cyber-bullying-not-as-concerning-as-facetoface-for-kids-study-20150310-13zx7y

17. Dillon, K. P., & Bushman, B. J. (2015). Unresponsive or un-noticed? Cyber-bystander intervention in an experimental cyberbullying context. *Computers in Human Behavior, 45*, 144–150.

18. Desai, A. N. (2015, February 26). Online trolls, cyber-bullying succeeds because no one intervenes or stands-up against the bullies, prove scientists. *The Inquisitr*. Retrieved from http://www.inquisitr.com/1876523/cyber-bullying-succeeds

19. You can watch the video on YouTube at https://www.youtube.com/watch?v=EisZTB4ZQxY

20. Hinduja, S., & Patchin, J. W. (2015). *Bullying beyond the schoolyard: Preventing and responding to cyberbullying* (2nd ed.). Thousand Oaks, CA: Corwin.

21. Duggan, M. (2015, August 19). Mobile messaging and social media 2015. *Pew Research Center*. Retrieved from http://www.pewinternet.org/2015/08/19/mobile-messaging-and-social-media-2015

22. Kessler, J. (2010, April 30). Principal to parents: Take kids off Facebook. *CNN*. Retrieved from http://www.cnn.com/2010/TECH/04/30/principal.facebook.ban/index.html

23. Finkelhor, D., Turner, H., Ormrod, R., & Hamby, S. L. (2010). Trends in childhood violence and abuse exposure. *Archives & Adolescent Medicine, 164*, 238–242; Jones, L. M., Mitchell, K. J., & Finkelhor, D. (2013). Online harassment in context: Trends from three youth Internet safety surveys (2000, 2005, 2010). *Psychology of Violence, 3*, 53–69. Retrieved from http://psycnet.apa.org/journals/vio/3/1/53

24. For more information, see Hinduja, S., & Patchin, J. W. (2012). Cyberbullying: Neither an epidemic nor a rarity. *European Journal of Developmental Psychology, 9*, 539–543.

25. Temkin, D. (2013, September 29). Stop saying bullying causes suicide. *The Huffington Post*. Retrieved from http://www.huffingtonpost.com/deborah-temkin/stop-saying-bullying-caus_b_4002897.html

26. Ibid.

27. Kim, Y. S., & Leventhal, B. (2008). Bullying and suicide. A review. *International Journal of Adolescent Medicine and Health, 20*, 133–154. Retrieved from http://www.ncbi.nlm.nih.gov/pubmed/18714552

28. Centers for Disease Control and Prevention. (2015). *Suicide: Risk and protective factors*. Retrieved from http://www.cdc.gov/ViolencePrevention/suicide/riskprotectivefactors.html

29. Hinduja, S., & Patchin, J. W. (2010). Bullying, cyberbullying, and suicide. *Archives of Suicide Research, 14*, 206–221.

30. Temkin, D. (2013, September 29). Stop saying bullying causes suicide. *The Huffington Post*. Retrieved from http://www.huffingtonpost.com/deborah-temkin/stop-saying-bullying-caus_b_4002897.html

31. Mitchell, K. J., Jones, L. M., Turner, H. A., Shattuck, A., & Wolak, J. (2015, June 1). The role of technology in peer harassment: Does it amplify harm for youth? *Psychology of Violence*. Advance online publication. doi:10.1037/a0039317

32. Hamaker, P. (2015, June 3). Study finds in-person bullying to be more harmful than cyberbullying. *Examiner*. Retrieved from http://www.examiner.com/article/study-finds-person-bullying-to-be-more-harmful-than-cyberbullying

33. Mitchell, K. J., Jones, L. M., Turner, H. A., Shattuck, A., & Wolak, J. (2015, June 1). The role of technology in peer harassment: Does it amplify harm for youth? *Psychology of Violence*. Advance online publication. doi:10.1037/a0039317

34. Ibid.

35. Cuadrado-Gordillo, I. (2012, July). Repetition, power imbalance, and intentionality: Do these criteria conform to teenagers' perception of bullying? A role-based analysis. *Journal of Interpersonal Violence, 27*, 1889–1910.

36. Patchin, J. W., & Hinduja, S. (2015). Measuring cyberbullying: Implications for research. *Aggression and Violent Behavior*, *23*, 69–74. Retrieved from http://www.sciencedirect.com/science/article/pii/S1359178915000750

37. Mitchell, K. J., Jones, L. M., Turner, H. A., Shattuck, A., & Wolak, J. (2015, June 1). The role of technology in peer harassment: Does it amplify harm for youth? *Psychology of Violence*. Advance online publication. doi:10.1037/a0039317

38. Bonanno, R. A., & Hymel, S. (2013). Cyber bullying and internalizing difficulties: Above and beyond the impact of traditional forms of bullying. *Journal of Youth and Adolescence*, *42*, 685–697.

39. Campbell, M., Spears, B., Slee, P., Butler, D., & Kift, S. (2012). Victims' perceptions of traditional and cyberbullying, and the psychosocial correlates of their victimisation. *Emotional and Behavioural Difficulties*, *17*, 389–401.

PART III

The Lowdown on Laws Related to Bullying

12

The Criminalization of Cyberbullying

Justin W. Patchin

I have written quite a bit over the years on our blog at cyberbullying.org on the question of whether it is necessary to enact new criminal statutes to combat cyberbullying. Be it a proposal for an amended state statute or a new city ordinance, it seems popular these days for politicians to publicly denounce cyberbullying and proffer legislation to make it a crime. Few stand on the side of those who mistreat others on Election Day, so it is probably a safe political platform. But is it the right approach?

A 2014 case out of Albany, New York, highlights some of the challenges of trying to enact practical cyberbullying legislation.[1] Back in 2011, a 15-year-old student was arrested and charged with a then recently passed county-level cyberbullying law. The student in this case was accused of creating a "flame page" wherein he posted photos and disparaging comments about a number of his classmates—some of which were sexual in nature. His attorney challenged the law as being overly broad, but lost in city court, and the student ultimately pled guilty (while still retaining the ability to appeal). He did appeal to the Albany County Court, but again lost. The New York State Court of Appeals then agreed to review the case.

Proponents of the law (and of the criminalization of bullying behaviors generally) say that those who bully others need to be held accountable, and if schools and parents can't—or won't—do it, then society should. Opponents see this law as an attack on free speech or challenge it as hastily written, with many essential elements left undefined or otherwise ambiguous. Others point out (quite rightly, in my opinion) that further criminalization will do little to solve the underlying causes of bullying overall.

In a 5–2 decision, the court stated that the cyberbullying ordinance that Albany County had drafted was poorly written and was therefore invalid. As drafted, the law was too broad and as a result violated the free speech clause of the First Amendment: *"It appears that the provision would criminalize a broad spectrum of speech outside the popular understanding of cyberbullying, including, for example: an email disclosing private information about a corporation or a telephone conversation meant to annoy an adult."*[2]

CYBERBULLYING IS NOT PROTECTED SPEECH

All U.S. citizens—even students—have a right to free expression. There are, of course, limitations to this. We simply don't have the right to say anything to anyone under any circumstances. Moreover, inasmuch as the content of the speech (what is being said) matters, so too do the context and consequences of that speech.

For example, as an alum of Michigan State University, it is perfectly fine for me to express my disdain for University of Michigan athletic teams. I can stand on a public park bench and proudly and loudly proclaim my hatred of the Wolverines. That is protected speech. But if I am a high school student and repeatedly express that view during the middle of algebra class—in a way that disrupts the learning environment at school—well, then, that speech, which was otherwise protected, is now subject to reasonable discipline. The school has long been recognized as a unique environment where extraordinary restrictions on speech and other forms of expression are allowed, when necessary, to uphold school rules and maintain an appropriate school climate. As noted in a 1986 U.S. Supreme Court opinion, "the undoubted freedom to advocate unpopular and controversial views in schools and classrooms must be balanced against the society's countervailing interest in teaching students the boundaries of socially appropriate behavior. . . . Nothing in the Constitution prohibits the states from insisting that certain modes of expression are inappropriate and subject to sanctions."[3] More recently, this interpretation has been expanded to include some student behaviors and speech expressed from beyond the school walls (to the extent they impact the school) (see Chapter 35).

Similarly, if I call someone up in the middle of the night and repeatedly, over the course of many weeks, tell him or her that "the Wolverines suck," that too may be subject to criminal sanction (for harassment or stalking). While the content of the speech is protected, the way in which it is conveyed is not. So, those tasked with keeping schools safe and orderly need to evaluate not only *what* was being said, but also *what impact* it had (or is likely to have) on the environment at school. Even speech that is protected in most circumstances could be subject to discipline under certain conditions.

While some have proclaimed the 2014 New York State Court of Appeals decision as a victory for free speech advocates and argued that the opinion confirms that criminalizing cyberbullying is not allowable, that is far from what the opinion really says.[4] In fact, the court was careful to specify that proscription of the behavior in question is possible if a law can be more precisely crafted:

> *Cyberbullying is not conceptually immune from government regulation, so we may assume, for the purposes of this case, that the First Amendment permits the prohibition of cyberbullying directed at children, depending on how that activity is defined.*[5]

We can set aside for a moment the question of whether new criminal statutes will help us solve the cyberbullying problem. I don't believe they will contribute much, and expect that other measures are likely to be much more effective. But, is the kind of speech the student promoted on Facebook protected? The court inferred that generally speaking, it is not.

The court acknowledged that most would agree that the student's behavior was *"repulsive and harmful to the subjects of his rants, and potentially created a risk of physical or emotional injury based on the private nature of the comments."*[6] Again, the court was concerned principally with the sloppy language of the law: *"Even if the First Amendment allows a cyberbullying statute of the limited nature proposed by Albany County, the local law here was not drafted in that manner."*[7]

ALTERNATIVES TO THE CRIMINAL JUSTICE SYSTEM

Generally speaking, I feel that the criminal justice system should be the absolute last resort when trying to resolve the vast majority of cyberbullying incidents. If a teen repeatedly targets a peer with hurtful, harassing, or malicious online insults, and family- and/or school-based responses prove ineffective, then perhaps law enforcement does need to get involved. Even with that, though, I would hope the police and prosecutor(s) would work to develop an appropriate solution that avoids a criminal stigma being placed on the teen.

> The criminal justice system should be the absolute last resort when trying to resolve the vast majority of cyberbullying incidents.

One option for responding to serious cyberbullying might be a deferred prosecution deal that is contingent on improved online behaviors. If the teen refrains from inappropriate online interactions for a specified period of time, then the charges would go away. Or maybe the accused could participate in a teen court, or meet with people who have been victimized by bullying in the past in a kind of restorative justice approach. Again, there are so many other possible avenues for dealing with bullying that hold much more promise for effectiveness than a misdemeanor criminal charge. All of these other options should be exhausted before requiring the teen to appear in front of a judge.

WHERE TO GO FROM HERE

So what kind of cyberbullying law language could pass constitutional muster? Well, there were some hints to this in the New York Court of Appeals opinion. Albany County's ordinance states:

> *Cyber-Bullying shall mean any act of communicating or causing a communication to be sent by mechanical or electronic means, including posting statements on the internet or through a computer or email network, disseminating embarrassing or sexually explicit photographs; disseminating private, personal, false or sexual information, or sending hate mail, with no legitimate private, personal, or public purpose, with the intent to harass, annoy, threaten, abuse, taunt, intimidate, torment, humiliate, or otherwise inflict significant emotional harm on another person.*[8]

As it stands, there are just a few specific words included that are problematic. In a dissenting opinion, Judge Robert Smith argued that a cyberbullying law should be clear to apply only to students (as written, Albany's ordinance seemingly applied also to adults and even possibly corporations). I'm not sure why Judge Smith believes that adults are immune from prosecution for their inappropriate online behaviors, but he seems to think they should be. There are also certain ambiguous terms that would need to be removed:

> *The County concedes that the words "embarrassing" and "hate mail" are "vague and thus unenforceable." . . . Once these deletions are made, I see nothing in the law that renders it unconstitutional.*[9]

So Albany County has gone back to the drawing board. County executive Daniel McCoy said that they would work "to craft a (new) law that both protects free speech and keep[s] kids safe."[10] Many other communities around the United States are likely in the same boat. While this ruling technically applies only to the state of New York, lawmakers in other communities would be advised to review their recently passed laws to make sure they can withstand the scrutiny applied to this law.

QUESTIONS FOR REFLECTION

Does your city or county have a cyberbullying law? If so, would it withstand legal scrutiny, based on lessons learned in this case? If not, could you draft a law that would be upheld by the courts? Should students be allowed to criticize their classmates (or teachers) when away from school?

13

SHOULD CITIES HAVE A CYBERBULLYING ORDINANCE?

Justin W. Patchin

I have received quite a few inquiries in the last several months from local elected officials interested in proposing a city or county ordinance to address cyberbullying (as Albany County discussed in Chapter 12 attempted to do). An ordinance is basically a law or legal decree passed by a local municipality (usually a city, township, or county) that has the authority of law within its geographical limits. For example, most cities have ordinances that govern parking, prohibit loud noises from vehicles, specify building standards, or require the licensure of pets. If one is found to be in violation of a municipal ordinance, the person is usually fined a relatively small amount of money.

Several cities in my home state of Wisconsin have recently passed ordinances (e.g., Viroqua[11] and Franklin[12]). In addition, a number of cities in Missouri enacted local ordinances prohibiting cyberbullying following the tragic suicide of Megan Meier in 2006.[13] At that time, there appeared to be very few legal (criminal) options to hold someone accountable for cyberbullying or other forms of online harassment. The question to consider is whether a local cyberbullying ordinance is the right way to tackle this problem. Here are my thoughts on this issue.

ORDINANCES MAY BE UNNECESSARY

All 50 states now have bullying laws in place, and the vast majority of those (48) include provisions related to electronic forms of harassment. The wording in these laws differs significantly from state to state, but all (except Montana) require schools to have policies in place to prohibit bullying, and most prescribe school-based sanctions for participating in bullying. So these laws and a long line of court case law states that cyberbullying that occurs on school property or that substantially disrupts the school environment is subject to school authority and discipline.

In addition, many states already have statewide criminal statutes that address cyberbullying. For example, in Wisconsin, it is a Class B misdemeanor to send an e-mail or other computerized communication "with intent to frighten, intimidate, threaten, abuse or harass" another person.[14] Moreover, individuals are subject to a fine of up to $1,000 if they "harass, annoy or offend another person" using an electronic communication system.[15] Very few law enforcement officers with whom I have spoken in Wisconsin have charged a student with violating this statute; however, it is slightly more common for the police in that state (and in other places around the United States) to charge a student with disorderly conduct for harassing online behaviors.

ORDINANCES MAY OFFER ALTERNATIVES TO STATE SANCTIONS

Overall, we need to ask ourselves, "What cyberbullying behaviors or scenarios exist that would not be covered under the above avenues and therefore would require a local ordinance?" I suppose if you are in a state that does not have suitable state bullying or harassment (online or otherwise) statutes, then pursuing a local remedy might be necessary. Some of the local officials have indicated to me that their county-level district attorney was reluctant or unwilling to file formal charges for cyberbullying behaviors, and a city ordinance would give local police the ability to go after individuals who engage in cyberbullying through the city attorney's office. I'm not convinced this is the best place to handle these cases, but it does provide an additional lever to pull for someone who continues to engage in problematic online behaviors.

If states had practical cyberbullying legislation, then local communities would not need to be looking to develop their own legal responses. I spend a lot of time working with legislators to develop cyberbullying laws. I advocate language that emphasizes the school's recognized authority to discipline students for *any* behavior that interferes with another student's ability to feel safe and to learn at school. Specifically, I encourage legislators to adopt the following language:

> *Schools have the authority and responsibility to apply reasonable and educationally based discipline, consistent with a pupil's constitutionally granted privileges, to bullying that (a) occurs on, or is delivered to, school property or a school-sponsored activity or event on or off school property or (b) occurs off of school property or outside of a school-sponsored activity or event if the conduct interferes with a pupil's educational opportunities, creates a hostile environment for that pupil or others, or substantially disrupts the orderly operations of the school or school-sponsored activity or event.*

To be sure, this language focuses exclusively on the *school's* role in responding to student bullying and cyberbullying. It is also vitally important that parents are involved in disciplining their children when they misuse technology, but that is more difficult to legislate. There is one other potential benefit to local ordinances that may be specific to Wisconsin (it may apply to other states—I just don't know). In Wisconsin, any contact that a person 17 years of age or older has with a circuit court (the state's lower-level criminal court) is listed online through the Consolidated Court Automation Programs website (www.wicourts.gov/courts/offices/ccap.htm). Anyone can look up others online through this public record system by name and birthdate to see what trouble they have gotten into. When screening applicants for jobs, it is easy for hiring managers to look in this database to see whether someone has had a brush with the law. For example, if a high school junior received an underage drinking ticket when she was 17 years old, that would be listed on this website. Forever. So if that same student was then issued a citation for misusing a computerized communication system (e.g., sending a harassing e-mail to a peer), a violation of Wisconsin state law, that too would be listed seemingly forever. If you are a victim of cyberbullying, then maybe you think this is a good thing: the one doing the bullying gets the punishment he or she deserves. But I think it is unrealistic to assume that anyone, especially teens, will be deterred from cyberbullying others for fear of being arrested and put on this online court system (see Chapter 24).

> It is unrealistic to assume that anyone, especially teens, will be deterred from cyberbullying others for fear of being arrested and put on this online court system.

This is where a local ordinance *might* be useful. If a city has a municipal ordinance prohibiting online harassment and also has a municipal court, then potentially the infraction will be handled at the local level, and therefore the citation will not end up in the online public record. The aggressor will still be punished, but it won't necessarily leave a lifetime impact like a state violation could.

The bottom line for me in all of this is that I believe that the vast majority of cyberbullying incidents, at least those that occur among school-aged youth, can and should be handled at the local level: by parents working with schools to resolve the situation outside of the formal juvenile justice system. If the harassment is particularly egregious or continues after attempts have been made to stop it, then perhaps additional formal steps are necessary. But I just think a local ordinance, on balance, will not do much to add to the tool kit of suitable response strategies for this problem.

QUESTIONS FOR REFLECTION

Does it make sense for cities to pass their own cyberbullying laws? Does your state bullying law have shortcomings that a local provision could address?

14

CELL PHONE SEARCHES

Implications for Educators
From *Riley v. California*

Justin W. Patchin

New insight about the issues associated with authorities searching the contents of cell phones has been provided by the U.S. Supreme Court. While this particular ruling deals specifically with the question of whether *law enforcement officers* can search the contents of cell phones possessed by people who are under arrest, *educators* can certainly learn from it as well.[16] In the opinion released in June 2014, the Court analyzed two separate incidents (one in California[17] and another in Massachusetts[18]) where officers searched—without a warrant—the cell phones of individuals they had arrested. In both cases, the phones revealed incriminating evidence that was used at trial, and both defendants were convicted.

THE SKINNY ON SEARCH AND SEIZURE

As a very rough and brief primer on basic criminal procedure law (don't take this as legal advice!), the police are allowed to search the contents of, for example, a bag that a person is carrying under a variety of circumstances. First, an officer may simply ask for permission to search it. If this isn't granted, but the officer has reason to believe that the bag contains evidence of a crime, the officer may seize it, and obtain a search warrant from a judge. The judge will review the available evidence and determine if a search is appropriate. If the officer feels that time is of the essence, and that waiting to obtain a warrant could create a public safety risk (e.g., if the bag is thought to contain a bomb), then a warrant is not needed for the search (referred to as "exigent circumstances"). The officer *will* be required to convince a judge of this necessity after the fact in order for any evidence obtained to be admissible in court.

There is another fairly common circumstance under which a person's bag can be searched without a warrant, permission, or exigent circumstances. Once a person is under arrest, everything on his or her person and anything within the area of his or her immediate reach is subject to search.[19] The purpose here is to identify weapons or evidence of a crime that may have been stashed by the accused upon hearing that the police were at hand. It is this latter scenario that was evaluated by the court in the current opinion: Can cell phones be searched, without a warrant, once a person has been arrested?

CELL PHONES ARE DIFFERENT

Some have argued that a cell phone is, in essence, no different from a bag: It contains "stuff," including possible evidence of a crime. And the rules, therefore, should be the same. If you are under arrest, the logic goes, your cell phone should be eligible to be searched (at least that's the way the cops in California and Massachusetts interpreted the law). In the end, the Court unanimously disagreed with this interpretation and ruled that cell phones are different from other items (such as briefcases or purses) and therefore are subject to different rules.

It was reasoned that cell phones have the potential to contain *so much* information, locally on the device but also remotely through cloud storage and Internet access, that the risk of invading one's personal privacy is too great to allow a search without reasonable justification. And even then it is difficult, if not impossible, to put restrictions on what exactly is searchable. Text messages? Personal contacts? Photos? Videos? Notes? Just being arrested shouldn't result in a person having to reveal everything about his or her life that is on, or connected to, his or her cell phone.

> Search of a cell phone is not *automatically* allowed when someone is arrested. There must be exigent circumstances or probable cause that the phone contains evidence of a crime.

To be clear, the Court did not say that searches of cell phones are completely off-limits. Rather, it ruled that a search is not *automatically* allowed when someone is arrested. There must be exigent circumstances or probable cause that the phone contains evidence of a crime.

IMPLICATIONS FOR EDUCATORS

So how does this ruling apply to educators? Well, it really doesn't. Nothing included in the language of the ruling suggests a change in law or policy concerning the circumstances under which it is appropriate for educators to search the contents of student-owned cell phones (or other portable electronic devices, for that matter) that are brought to school. We know that the rules that govern police officer behaviors are different from those that apply to educators (see Chapter 32). My review of the relevant case law leads me to conclude that educators can in fact search student cell phones under *very restricted* circumstances, but the parameters for such an action are not well specified, and it can be difficult for most educators to determine when a search is necessary and appropriate.

In another case, the U.S. Supreme Court stated that students are protected from unreasonable searches, but also that the standard required by law enforcement officers (probable cause of a crime) is not the same for educators.[20] School officials generally need only show that the search was "justified at its inception and reasonable in scope." What makes a search justified? What is reasonable? The greatest legal minds debate the answers to these questions, so how on earth are we to hope that a school administrator can accurately sort it all out? It is likely that many of these questions will end up being resolved in a courtroom at some point, but it is best to keep yourself and your school out of it.

We have produced a basic checklist that educators can use to help determine if a search is reasonable and justified in their particular situation (see cyberbullying.org/cell-phone-search-checklist-for-school-administrators/). But again, these standards have not been tested in a court of law, so they are only speculative at this point. Our best advice to educators is to resist searching a student-owned cell phone unless there is a possible safety concern (e.g., a student says that she just received a text message from another student who said he has a gun). And in this kind of situation, it is best to turn the case over to law enforcement officers, who should better understand the current legal framework for these circumstances. More importantly, it is advised that educators discuss these issues with their school resource/liaison officer and school district attorney so

> Resist searching a student-owned cell phone unless there is a possible safety concern.

that everyone is more or less on the same page. Don't wait until you are confronting a student who is believed to have contraband content on his phone to develop appropriate procedures.

QUESTIONS FOR REFLECTION

What is your school policy for searching student-owned mobile devices? Have you discussed your procedures with local law enforcement or the prosecutor's office?

15

EDUCATOR SEARCHES OF PRIVATE STUDENT SOCIAL MEDIA PROFILES

The Illinois Experiment

Justin W. Patchin

In the summer of 2014, Illinois (somewhat quietly) passed a new bullying law that took effect on January 1, 2015.[21] The law includes language, similar to at least 13 other states' laws, that makes it clear that schools have the authority to discipline students for cyberbullying that occurs off campus (and outside of a school-sponsored activity) when such behavior substantially disrupts their educational processes or orderly operation. This has been the long-held federal standard, and I was happy to see Illinois moving in the right direction (see also Minnesota's recent update, discussed in Chapter 19).

About the time this law was signed by the governor of Illinois, a former educator from that state told me about another aspect of the law that seemed to permit educators to demand passwords to private social media profiles of students suspected of inappropriate online behaviors impacting the school. I looked into it more, and it turns out that this comes from a separate law that actually took effect on January 1, 2014 (over a year before the latest law).[22] The 2015 law perhaps amplified the implications of the earlier provision with its focus on off-campus behaviors. But why did it take so long for the public to notice it?

ILLINOIS LAW

The controversial law begins with a provision that appears to expressly prohibit *postsecondary* schools (it doesn't mention elementary or secondary schools) from requesting password information from students or parents:

> *(a) It is unlawful for a post-secondary school to request or require a student or his or her parent or guardian to provide a password or other related account information in order to gain access to the student's account or profile on a social networking website or to demand access in any manner to a student's account or profile on a social networking website.*[23]

But when one reads it more closely, the law also seems to create a loophole that would apparently allow educators to demand passwords in special circumstances (or at least not prohibit it):

> *(d) This Section does not apply when a post-secondary school has reasonable cause to believe that a student's account on a social networking website contains evidence that the student has violated a school disciplinary rule or policy.*[24]

So which is it? Can schools request (or demand) this personal information or not? And does this apply only to postsecondary schools and not to K–12 schools?

FEDERAL LAW

It is true that students have different privacy expectations while at school. Courts have allowed school officials to search for weapons or drugs in school-owned lockers, for example.[25] They've also supported the school's ability to "search" a student for drug use by randomly testing student athletes or others involved in extracurricular activities.[26]

In *New Jersey v. T.L.O.* (1985), the U.S. Supreme Court addressed school searches of *student-owned property* at school. The Court specifically examined whether a school official can search a student's purse when there is reasonable suspicion that the purse contains evidence of a violation of school policy (in the case of T.L.O., cigarettes). The Court affirmed that

> *schoolchildren have legitimate expectations of privacy . . . But striking the balance between [that] and the school's equally legitimate need to maintain an environment in which learning can take place requires some easing of the restrictions to which searches by public authorities are ordinarily subject.*[27]

In short, "the legality of a search of a student should depend simply on the reasonableness, under all the circumstances, of the search." Ultimately, the Court supported the search of the purse, ruling that it was reasonable given what was known at the time.

STUDENT SEARCHES IN THE 21ST CENTURY

I have previously analyzed the case law as it relates to searches of student-owned cell phones,[28] and wrote about lessons that can be learned from the 2014 Supreme Court case *Riley v. California*, which restricts law enforcement access to cell phones (see Chapter 14). All things considered, I think it is safe to conclude that courts are generally inclined to err on the side of privacy when it comes to prying into personal digital data and private profiles. Students do generally have an expectation of privacy concerning the content of their private social media profiles, but exigent circumstances *can* mean that access to the profile is warranted. If, for instance, a reliable student reports to school officials that a classmate has made a bomb threat online or is talking of suicide, then time is of the essence, and I suspect the courts would allow educators or the police to demand the necessary information for their investigation.

But what if a student posts the answers to an exam on a private profile? Or criticizes a teacher or teases a classmate? These behaviors surely "violate a school's disciplinary rule or policy," but are they covered by the law?

> Courts are generally inclined to err on the side of privacy when it comes to prying into personal digital data and private profiles.

In 2014, a Minnesota school agreed to pay $70,000 in damages (without admitting liability) to settle a lawsuit in which it was accused of invading a sixth-grader's privacy by demanding that she turn over the passwords to her e-mail and Facebook profile.[29] Originally, the student was given detention and forced to write a letter of apology for making disparaging remarks online about an adult hall monitor. When she returned to Facebook to vent her frustration and try to find out "who the F%$#" told on her, she was suspended (in school) for insubordination. In a later incident, someone reported to the school that this same student had been communicating online with a classmate in a sexually inappropriate way. When interviewed by a counselor at the school, she admitted to saying "naughty" things to the classmate, but that it occurred off campus and after school hours. School officials and a police officer then demanded her Facebook and e-mail passwords so they could look into it. She initially refused, but school officials threatened her with detention, and she eventually complied.

It's important to acknowledge that the outcome of this case was a *settlement*, not a court order. So we really don't know how a judge or jury would have felt about the school's actions. I personally think that the school was well within its rights to discipline the student for the inappropriate online comments about the hall monitor and the subsequent insubordination. Where the school went astray, in my opinion, was when the administrators forced the student to turn over her passwords without evidence of an imminent threat to herself or others. It is unreasonable for a school, or a police officer, to demand access to private communications absent those standards. If a social media profile is open to the public, however, then it is very likely fair game for anyone to review. But just because schools can look doesn't mean they should (see Chapter 23).

SO WHERE DOES THIS LEAVE US?

The Illinois law has gained notoriety at a time when at least a dozen other states have enacted legislation to *prohibit* employers or universities from demanding passwords from employees or students.[30] If nothing else, Illinois is clearly bucking the trend. That said, this law has apparently been on the books for over a year, yet I am not aware of any schools that have attempted to apply it. It's also unclear whether it actually applies to elementary, middle, and high schools at all. The law does seem to require primary and secondary schools to notify students and parents that access to student-created social media pages may be necessary during the course of a school investigation, but it doesn't explicitly state that schools have the authority to *demand* access to *private* profiles.

If I were a parent and a school official requested that my child turn over the password to his or her private online profile, I would refuse to do so without police officer presence and a warrant (or at least not without being present myself). Of course, if there was legitimate cause for concern about the safety of my child or another, I would immediately review the profile myself, with my child, to evaluate the potential threat. Relevant information would then be turned over to the authorities as appropriate. I would also remind my children to double-check that all of their social media profiles are restricted (i.e., set to "private") so that only those they accept as friends or followers can view the information. They should similarly ensure their cell phone is locked with a passcode.

If I were an educator, I would be extremely cautious when it comes to situations where I might invade a student's privacy. Again, the law gives schools some latitude here, but schools really need to make the case for why the intrusion is necessary given the circumstances. If I had a bona fide concern about the safety of a student or staff member, it would be worth the risk. Short of that, I'm not sure. What is "reasonable" to one person might not be to another. And if that other person is a judge, it could spell trouble for the school. I have no doubt that this law will eventually be challenged. Here's hoping it doesn't involve you or your school.

QUESTIONS FOR REFLECTION

Should schools be allowed to require that students turn over passwords to private profiles or passcodes to locked cell phones? What are the pros and cons of such activities? Have educators at your school searched the contents of private sites or phones?

16

MINNESOTA'S NEW BULLYING LAW AND THE ABILITY OF EDUCATORS TO RESPOND TO OFF-CAMPUS BULLYING

Justin W. Patchin

On April 9, 2014, Minnesota governor Mark Dayton signed into law the Safe and Supportive Minnesota Schools Act, which, among other things, updates the state's anti-bullying legislation.[31] The previous version of the law, last updated in 2007, was much maligned as being among the "worst in the nation." I'm not sure that designation is accurate, but it was by far the *shortest* bullying law in the United States at just 37 words. The new law is much more comprehensive, which is perhaps one reason it has attracted its share of critics.

Some argue that it is an attack on local control or that it somehow challenges the ability of parents to respond to bullying in a way that they think is appropriate. Others say it threatens free speech. Still others argue that this is just another unfunded mandate for schools (and, to that claim, I say, "Fair enough"). I am concerned that it appears that no additional resources are being allocated to schools to implement the new provisions. This is unfortunately an all-too-common element of new statutes that have been passed across the country (see, especially, New Jersey's bullying law).[32]

ADDRESSING OFF-CAMPUS BULLYING

One other aspect of the new Minnesota law that seems to be attracting criticism is the provision that specifies that schools are entitled to discipline students for bullying, even if the bullying didn't occur at school. The section of the new law that is most relevant to this reads as follows:

Student bullying policy; scope and application. (a) This section applies to bullying by a student against another student enrolled in a public school and which occurs:

(1) *on the school premises, at the school functions or activities, or on the school transportation;*

(2) *by use of electronic technology and communications on the school premises, during the school functions or activities, on the school transportation, or on the school computers, networks, forums, and mailing lists;*

(3) *by use of electronic technology and communications off the school premises to the extent such use substantially and materially disrupts student learning or the school environment;*[33]

This is an issue we have written about at length, and Chapter 35 summarizes the current case law regarding this question. But I wanted to briefly clarify what schools can and can't do when it comes to responding to off-campus student speech. Students from a University of Minnesota Law School course titled "Student Speech: Rights and Regulations" wrote an editorial commentary that was published in the Minneapolis *Star Tribune* where they highlight some of the issues.[34] I had the privilege of discussing free speech as it relates to teen cyberbullying with this class just before the editorial was published, so I was happy to learn that the students were weighing in publicly on this discussion. Their underlying concern seems to be that the law in this area is far from settled and that the new bullying law may be setting up schools for legal challenges, especially if they discipline students for off-campus behaviors.

In their commentary, the law students assert that "there is general agreement that public school students have First Amendment rights, but little consensus on how to address student bullying that occurs online at home." Indeed, students do in fact have First Amendment rights, including the right to free expression. But it is important to clarify that *many* court cases have demonstrated that those rights are curtailed significantly while at school, or to the extent the expressions significantly impact what is going on at school.[35]

Courts have also upheld the ability of schools to discipline students for their off-campus expressions.[36] The key issue in these types of cases is whether the off-campus speech resulted in, or has a foreseeable likelihood of resulting in, a substantial disruption of the learning environment at school.[37] In cases where courts have agreed with school officials that a substantial disruption existed or was imminent, their authority to discipline was upheld. The only cases I am aware of where schools lost at court was when they disciplined students on the extreme end of the punishment continuum (long-term suspension or expulsion) without being able to articulate and prove a disruption at school.[38] I'm not aware of a single case where a court at any level agreed that a disruption at school had occurred and yet still ruled against the school. That is to say not that it hasn't happened, just that it hasn't happened in a court at a level that matters for the purposes of a national discussion.

> In cases where courts have agreed with school officials that a substantial disruption existed or was imminent, their authority to discipline was upheld.

And even in cases where schools have overstepped their authority by punishing students for nondisruptive off-campus behaviors, the courts have been careful to state that their rulings do not close the door to all possible instances where a school would be correct to respond.[39] The law students are correct, however, that the issue of off-campus online speech has not yet been *directly* addressed by the U.S. Supreme Court (though the Court has declined to review at least three cases where lower courts have returned mixed interpretations).

MINNESOTA LAW IS NOT UNIQUE

It should also be noted that statutory language like that included in the Minnesota law is not completely new. At least a dozen other states across the United States have updated their anti-bullying statutes to explicitly allow schools to discipline students for their off-campus behaviors when (as discussed above) said behaviors infringe on the rights of other students or substantially and materially disrupt the learning environment at school (or have the likelihood of doing so). For example, New Hampshire law states that

*bullying or cyberbullying shall occur when an action or communication . . .
[o]ccurs off of school property or outside of a school-sponsored
activity or event, if the conduct interferes with a pupil's educational
opportunities or substantially disrupts the orderly operations of the
school or school-sponsored activity or event.*[40]

Tennessee law allows for discipline

*if the act takes place off school property or outside of a school-
sponsored activity, it is directed specifically at a student or students
and has the effect of creating a hostile educational environment or
otherwise creating a substantial disruption to the education environment or learning process.*[41]

These provisions are consistent with existing case law, and I am not aware
of any current legal challenges to these statutes.

So my perspective is that *we do in fact have some clarity*, in that we do
know that there are circumstances where schools are well within their rights
to discipline students for certain off-campus behaviors. I do fear that we may
be asking too much of school adminis-
trators in requiring that they are able to
clearly distinguish those off-campus
behaviors that result in a substantial
disruption at school from those that
don't. It would have been nice if the
Minnesota legislature had clarified what exactly "substantial disruption" means
(some states have—see laws in California and Arkansas[42]). For now, we simply encourage educators to apply reasonable sanctions when they believe it to
be necessary to stop the bullying behaviors. The only time they are likely to
be sued is if they are deliberately indifferent to bullying (they ignore it even
after it's brought to their attention) or if they respond in an overly harsh manner (expulsion or long-term suspension). Reasonableness is generally under-
stood and accepted by the courts.

> Apply reasonable sanctions when
> you believe it to be necessary to
> stop bullying behaviors.

QUESTIONS FOR REFLECTION

*Under what circumstances do you still feel confused or uncomfor-
table disciplining students who bully others via actions that
originate away from campus? What restrictions should be placed
on educators when it comes to addressing off-campus incidents?*

17

Bullying, Students With Disabilities, and Federal Law

Sameer Hinduja

At a conference in Chester County, Pennsylvania, in 2015, I had the privilege of getting to know Andy Faust, who is an authority on special education law at Sweet, Stevens, Katz, & Williams.[43] In particular, I was impressed by his level of expertise and intrigued by his astute observations about the Individuals with Disabilities Education Act (IDEA) and how some kids who are bullied—and some kids who bully others—may be entitled to the federal law's protections as "children with disabilities." I told Andy that no one is really talking about the reality and implications of this in my circles, and that it is worth discussing and sharing so that they can fully understand the situation. So, he and I went back and forth a few times to try to flesh this out.

Basically, Andy pointed out that many kids who are regularly involved in bullying behaviors (as aggressors or targets) can be classified as "children with disabilities" according to IDEA. When these youth act out in severe or chronic ways, they arguably meet the definition of *severely emotionally disturbed* (SED). This is one of 12 disability categories under which students can qualify for special education services. Notably, the definition of SED

> Many kids who are regularly involved in bullying behaviors (as aggressors or targets) can be classified as "children with disabilities" according to IDEA.

requires that the child in question demonstrate any one of five separate "characteristics" to a "marked degree and over a long period of time."[44]

Among those characteristics are the following:

- 2.08 (3) (a) (i) An inability to learn which is not primarily the result of intellectual, sensory or other health factors
- 2.08 (3) (a) (ii) An inability to build or maintain interpersonal relationships which significantly interferes with the child's social development
- 2.08 (3) (a) (iii) Inappropriate types of behavior or feelings under normal circumstances
- 2.08 (3) (a) (iv) A general pervasive mood of unhappiness or depression
- 2.08 (3) (a) (v) A tendency to develop physical symptoms or fears associated with personal or school problems[45]

It is reasonable to view this list of characteristics as behaviors we might consider bullying. To note, though, there is a so-called socially maladjusted rule—out in the SED definition—which basically means that you cannot state that a child is SED if this is the case. Well, you might wonder exactly what *socially maladjusted* means. Even though the term has no resonance in modern clinical practice, it is one that many associate with conduct disorder or sociopathic behavior, and therefore ultimately subject to interpretation.[46]

The problem with all of this is that one cannot easily discriminate between behavior that is "inappropriate . . . under ordinary circumstances" and that which is socialized in the child, or is a conscious source of pleasure or positive reinforcement for the child, when he or she bullies others.[47] We are therefore left to try to figure out whether those who bully are intentionally hurtful toward others, or if their bullying behavior simply stems from the fact that they are possibly SED (see the bullet-pointed characteristics above). If the former, those who bully others do not qualify for special education services because they are *socially maladjusted. However, the reality is that some kids are not intentionally hurtful but act out and bully others as a mechanism to cope with the fact they are SED. This means that they are therefore deserving of special education services.*

On the other side of the equation, many bullying *targets* also can readily demonstrate one or more of the SED characteristics "to a marked degree and over a long period of time."[48] As stated earlier, these include "inappropriate type[s] of behavior under ordinary circumstances," "an inability to develop or maintain satisfactory relationships with peers or adults," and "fears or anxiety associated with school or other issues."[49] As such, demonstrating these symptoms in sufficient severity warrants their classification under the SED label—*rendering them due special education services* under IDEA. As another outcome, some kids who are bullied also can act out not just as a coping mechanism, but possibly because they have or develop autism spectrum disorder (ASD).[50] Autism is, of course, another one of the 12 labels available under IDEA for classification of students in need (and deserving) of special education services.

Andy also brought up an important point: exactly *what* are bullied youth—and youth who bully others—entitled to as it relates to special education interventions if they are considered to be students with disabilities? Under IDEA, the purpose of special education is not just correction and support of *academic* deficits. Indeed, *social* and *behavioral* deficits that affect participation in the learning process or access to the learning environment are regarded in much the same way as an academic deficit. Basically, we have to teach children with learning-interfering behaviors the techniques to help them: become more self-aware and identify environments and situations that prompt attitudinal and behavioral struggles; self-monitor negative thoughts and emotions stemming from stress triggers in their lives; control their inclination to act out; and replace negative feelings with neutral or positive ones as they engage in self-management.

Of course, we must also teach youth with social skills deficits to recognize nonverbal social cues and the meaning of colloquial and idiomatic language (so they don't take certain statements expressed by their peers too seriously or literally) and to initiate and sustain appropriate conversations with peers and adults. These outcomes can be described and monitored measurably as annual goals in an individualized education program (IEP) and implemented through direct, explicit instruction in a special education classroom.[51] Alternatively, they can be implemented in the form of a "related service" such as general counseling, psychological and mental health counseling, and social work services—either delivered one-on-one or in a group setting.

In closing, Andy pointed out that special education is an intervention of extraordinary last resort. It seems wisest to move to a special education solution for those kids who are bullied or who bully others *who are already diagnosed and identified as disabled* and whose behavior is a manifestation of their identified disabilities. For those children *not* diagnosed and identified as such, we should employ general intervention practices to provide various types of measurable, outcomes-driven support (such as that described above).

While I was digging deeper to understand all of the issues involved, I had a follow-up chat with my colleague and friend, Americans with Disabilities Act (ADA) attorney Mike Tully.[52] When it can be shown certain behaviors are a result of a formally diagnosed impairment (bipolarity, obsessive-compulsive disorder [OCD], attention deficit/hyperactivity disorder [ADHD], anxiety disorder, depression, oppositional defiant disorder [ODD], etc.), schools are legally responsible to provide accommodation instead of discipline for the aggressors and additional services/support for the targets. *Schools cannot discipline a disability, nor can they discipline and provide accommodations at the same time.*

Parents of aggressors and targets *can* lobby for additional support, services, and resources for their kids under the auspices of IDEA, but schools should make sure a formal medical diagnosis is made to avoid overidentification. This would be detrimental because (a) public schools have little resources to go around as it is and (b) there is a history of placing African American males in special education programming simply because they tend to be more hyperactive (and this constitutes a form of segregation).[53] Also, there is a need to protect against false claims that a student is SED and thereby a qualifier for special privileges and services. To reiterate, only if a child is *formally diagnosed* as suffering from a disability should we proceed in providing him or her with IDEA-related accommodations so that the student can have educational opportunities without compromise. Furthermore, only then should that diagnosis change a school's traditional response to the student's involvement in bullying as the offender or target.

QUESTIONS FOR REFLECTION

In what systematic and programmatic ways does your school come to the support of those who bully others? Is that population neglected while the focus has been on supporting targets? Have you dealt with any claims related to IDEA, and are you prepared to accommodate students according to its provisions?

ENDNOTES

1. Hale-Spencer, M. (2014, June 6). State's top court questions efficacy of cyber-bullying law. *The Altamont Enterprise Guilderland*. Retrieved from http://www.altamontenterprise.com/news/guilderland/06062014/states-top-court-questions-efficacy-cyberbullying-law

2. *People v. Marquan M.*, 24 N.Y.3d 1, 9 (2014). Page 11. Retrieved from http://www.nycourts.gov/ctapps/Decisions/2014/Jul14/139opn14-Decision.pdf; see p. 11.

3. *Bethel School District No. 403 v. Fraser*, 478 U.S. 675 (1986).

4. New York's highest court says cyberbullying criminal law goes too far. (2014, July 1). New York Civil Liberties Union. Retrieved from http://www.nyclu.org/news/nys-highest-court-says-cyberbullying-criminal-law-goes-too-far

5. *People v. Marquan M.*, 24 N.Y.3d 1 (2014). Retrieved from http://www.nycourts.gov/ctapps/Decisions/2014/Jul14/139opn14-Decision.pdf; see p. 8.

6. Ibid., p. 15.

7. Ibid., p. 14.

8. Local law no. 11 for 2010: A local law prohibiting cyber-bullying in Albany County (2010, July 12). Retrieved from http://www.albanycounty.com/Libraries/Crime_Victims_and_Sexual_Violence_Center/LocalLaw_No_11_for_2010_CyberBullying.sflb.ashx

9. *People v. Marquan M.*, 24 N.Y.3d 1 (2014). Retrieved from http://www.nycourts.gov/ctapps/Decisions/2014/Jul14/139opn14-Decision.pdf

10. Wiessner, D. (2014, July 1). N.Y. top court says cyberbullying law violates free speech. *Reuters*. Retrieved from http://www.reuters.com/article/2014/07/01/us-new-york-cyberbully-idUSKBN0F64N420140701

11. Fenske, A. (2012, April 24). Cyber bullying ordinance passed in Viroqua. *Weau*. Retrieved from http://www.weau.com/home/headlines/Cyber_bullying_ordinance_passed_in_Viroqua_148754995.html

12. Romano, C. (2012, April 25). Franklin makes cyberbullying a crime. *Franklin Now*. Retrieved from http://www.franklinnow.com/news/148874525.html

13. Megan Meier case prompts cyberbullying ordinance in small Missouri town. (2008, March 5). *KSDK*. Retrieved from http://archive.ksdk.com/news/story.aspx?storyid=141601

14. Wisconsin Statutes. (2015, November 19). Chapter 947: Crimes against public peace, order and other interests. Retrieved from http://docs.legis.wisconsin.gov/statutes/statutes/947.pdf

15. Ibid.

16. *Riley v. California*, 573 U.S. ___ (2014). Retrieved from http://www.supremecourt.gov/opinions/13pdf/13-132_8l9c.pdf

17. Ibid.

18. *United States v. Wurie*, 573 U.S. ___ (573 U.S. 2014).

19. This authority stems from another case, *Chimel v. California*, 395 U.S. 752 (1969). Retrieved from http://caselaw.findlaw.com/us-supreme-court/395/752.html

20. *New Jersey v. T.L.O.*, 469 U.S. 325 (1985). Retrieved from https://www.law.cornell.edu/supremecourt/text/469/325

21. Public Act 098-0801: HB4207 enrolled. (2014–2015). Retrieved from http://www.ilga.gov/legislation/publicacts/98/PDF/098-0801.pdf

22. Right to Privacy in the School Setting Act (105 ILCS 75). (2014). Retrieved from http://www.ilga.gov/legislation/ilcs/ilcs3.asp?ActID=3504&ChapterID=17

23. Ibid.

24. Right to Privacy in the School Setting Act (105 ILCS 75) amendments. (2015, August 25). Retrieved from http://www.ilga.gov/legislation/publicacts/fulltext.asp?Name=099-0460.

25. National Center for Education Statistics. (1996, September). *Creating safe and drug-free schools: An action guide.* Washington, DC: U.S. Department of Education. Retrieved from https://www2.ed.gov/offices/OSDFS/actguid/searches.html

26. *Vernonia School District 47J v. Acton*, 515 U.S. 646 (1995); *Board of Education of Independent School District No. 92 of Pottawatomie County v. Earls*, 536 U.S. 822 (2002).

27. *New Jersey v. T.L.O.*, 469 U.S. 325 (1985). Retrieved from https://www.law.cornell.edu/supremecourt/text/469/325

28. Cyberbullying Research Center. (2011, February 10). When can educators search student cell phones? Retrieved from http://cyberbullying.org/when-can-educators-search-student-cell-phones

29. Brown, C. (2014, March 25). ACLU wins settlement for sixth-grader's Facebook posting. *Star Tribune.* Retrieved from http://www.startribune.com/minnewaska-student-wins-70k-from-school-over-facebook-post/252263751

30. Dame, Jonathan. (2014, January 10). Will employers still ask for Facebook passwords in 2014? *USA Today.* Retrieved from http://www.usatoday.com/story/money/business/2014/01/10/facebook-passwords-employers/4327739/

31. HF 826: Safe and Supportive Minnesota Schools Act. (2014). Retrieved from https://www.revisor.mn.gov/bills/text.php?session=ls88&number=HF826&session_number=0&session_year=2013&version=list

32. Patchin, Justin W. (2011, September 1). Another well-meaning, but unfunded mandate to address bullying. *Cyberbullying Research Center.* Retrieved from http://cyberbullying.org/another-well-meaning-but-unfunded-mandate-to-address-bullying/

33. HF 826: Safe and Supportive Minnesota Schools Act [emphasis added]. (2014). Retrieved from https://www.revisor.mn.gov/bills/text.php?session=ls88&number=HF826&session_number=0&session_year=2013&version=list

34. A gut check, please, on the Safe and Supportive Schools Act. (2014, April 2). *Star Tribune.* Retrieved from http://www.startribune.com/a-gut-check-please-on-the-safe-and-supportive-schools-act/253648041

35. For example, *Bethel School District No. 403 v. Fraser*, 478 U.S. 675 (1986); *Hazelwood School District et al. v. Kuhlmeier*, 484 U.S. 260 (1988).

36. For example, *Doninger v. Niehoff*, 527 F.3d 41 (2d Cir. 2008); *Fenton v. Stear*, 423 F.Supp. 767 (E.D. Pa. 1976); *J.S. v. Bethlehem Area School District*, 757 A.2d 412 (Pa. Commw. Ct. 2000); *Kowalski v. Berkeley County Schools*, 652 F.3d 565 (4th Cir. 2011); *Wisniewski v. Board of Education of the Weedsport Central School District*, 494 F.3d 34 (2d Cir. 2007).

37. See also *Barr v. Lafon*, 217 F. App'x 518 (6th Cir. 2007).

38. For example, *J.S. ex rel. Snyder v. Blue Mountain School District*, 650 F.3d 915 (3d Cir. 2011) (en banc); *Layshock v. Hermitage School District*, 412 F. Supp. 2d 502 (W.D. Pa. 2006).

39. *Tinker et al. v. Des Moines Independent Community School District et al.*, 393 U.S. 503 (1969); *Layshock v. Hermitage School District*, 593 F.3d 249 (3d Cir. 2010); *aff'd*, 650 F.3d 205 (3d Cir. 2011) (en banc). Retrieved from http://www.ca3.uscourts.gov/opinarch/074465p1.pdf and http://www2.ca3.uscourts.gov/opinarch/074465p1.pdf

40. Chapter 155: HB 1523—Final version. (2010). Retrieved from http://www.gencourt.state.nh.us/legislation/2010/hb1523.html

41. TN Code § 49-6-4502. (2014). Retrieved from http://law.justia.com/codes/tennessee/2014/title-49/chapter-6/part-45/section-49-6-4502

42. See http://cyberbullying.org/cyberbullying-laws/

43. Sweet, Stevens, Katz, & Williams. (2016). *Andrew E. Faust*. Retrieved from http://www.sweetstevens.com/attorneys/andrew-e-faust

44. Individuals with Disabilities Education Act, 20 U.S.C. § 1400 (2004).

45. NYC Department of Education. (2015). *Eligible categories of disability*. Retrieved from http://schools.nyc.gov/Academics/SpecialEducation/SEP/determination/eligible-categories-disability.htm

46. Smith, D. D. (2014, April 30). Emotional or behavioral disorders defined. *Education.com*. Retrieved from http://www.education.com/reference/article/emotional-behavioral-disorders-defined

47. NYC Department of Education, 2.08 (3) (a) (iii).

48. Individuals with Disabilities Education Act, 20 U.S.C. § 1400 (2004).

49. Ibid.

50. National Institute of Mental Health. (n.d.). *Autism spectrum disorder*. Retrieved from http://www.nimh.nih.gov/health/topics/autism-spectrum-disorders-asd/index.shtml

51. Baumel, J. (2010, February). What is an IEP? *Great Kids*. Retrieved from http://www.greatschools.org/special-education/legal-rights/513-what-is-an-iep.gs

52. French, Robert. (2015, November 25). Woolworths employee jailed over workplace bullying at Moe store. *News*. Retrieved from http://www.abc.net.au/news/2015-11-25/woolworths-employee-jailed-over-workplace-bullying-at-moe-store/6973828

53. NewsOne Now. (2015, April 16). ADHD wars against black boys: Dr. Umar Johnson details how to combat misdiagnosis of the learning disorder. *NewsOne*. Retrieved from http://newsone.com/3107853/adhd-misdiagnosis-black-boys-dr-umar-johnson

PART IV

Preventing Bullying Before It Starts

What You Can Do

18

NOTHING WORKS?

Taking Stock of America's "War on Bullying"

Justin W. Patchin

The Obama administration arguably declared war on bullying in the fall of 2010 when it convened the first federally supported Bullying Prevention Summit. In 2011, StopBullying.gov was launched. That same year, I attended a conference hosted by President Obama at the White House, where he said: "If there's one goal of this conference, it's to dispel the myth that bullying is just a harmless rite of passage or an inevitable part of growing up."[1] Since then, significant resources have been directed toward various programs and initiatives, resulting in what could be characterized as a "bullying industrial complex." Many companies now offer simple "solutions" to bullying. But are any of these efforts working?

LESSONS LEARNED FROM EFFORTS IN THE CRIMINAL JUSTICE SYSTEM

More than 40 years ago, sociologist Robert Martinson published an article that changed the course of history, or at least the history of the U.S. criminal justice system.[2] He quite appropriately sought to ascertain the effectiveness of programs that were being used to rehabilitate those among us who choose to break the law. Upon reviewing the available evaluation evidence, he came to the conclusion that, "with few and isolated exceptions, the rehabilitative efforts that have been reported so far have had no appreciable effect on recidivism."[3] This was subsequently converted by politicians and the media to a much more concise and headline-worthy "Nothing Works." If Twitter had been around back then, you can bet #NothingWorks would have been trending.

The reason this article, and its subsequent public interpretation, was historic can be easily seen in the impact it had on incarceration rates in the United States. In 1980, about 320,000 U.S. citizens were in prison. In 2013, that number was over 1.5 million. Between 1970 and 2010, the incarceration rate (number of people per 100,000) increased fivefold.[4]

Martinson's article has been credited as being the force that powerfully and almost instantaneously pushed the penal pendulum away from a medical model—focused on treating the underlying causes of a person's criminality—to a retributive regime wherein community safety and crime control became a top priority. The result was three decades of mass incarceration, fueled by mandatory sentencing schemes, and the abolition of release-readiness–determining parole boards. However, most people—even staunch tough-on-crime–minded folks—would agree that this policy has failed miserably, resulting in more crime, not less.[5] And that's to say nothing of the social and economic toll on society.

BULLYING PREVENTION EFFORTS IN 2015

Some could say that we are at another Martinson moment with respect to our efforts to curb bullying. The work of federal, state, and local governments has definitely prompted increased public discourse about bullying. Simultaneously, though, resource-strapped schools continue to struggle with heightened expectations that they "handle" these situations. Many educators have therefore turned to various bullying prevention programs, initiatives, and campaigns to make some headway in reducing the problem. Unfortunately, only a small handful of these efforts have been rigorously evaluated. And of those that

> Only a small handful of bullying prevention programs, initiatives, and campaigns have been rigorously evaluated.

have, many have been shown to fall short in making truly significant gains. If you believe the research, most of what we have done to prevent bullying since the mid-1990s has not yielded the kind of results we would hope for. University of Illinois psychologist Dorothy Espelage summarized the sentiment succinctly: "the impact of bullying prevention programs in the United States has been disappointing."[6]

Recent high-profile analyses of dozens of bullying prevention program evaluations have all generally come to the same conclusion: nothing works. Most troublingly, a study published in 2013 suggested that schools that have implemented a bullying prevention program *are actually doing worse* when it comes to preventing bullying than schools that have not—specifically, "students attending schools with bullying prevention programs were more likely to have experienced peer victimization, compared to those attending schools without bullying prevention programs."[7] This was picked up by the media and shared widely as evidence that bullying prevention programs do not work.

In this study, researchers examined data from 7,001 students from 195 schools across the United States. Of the schools, 65% had some bullying prevention program, presumably as reported by the students from within those schools. Students who said their school had a bullying prevention program were significantly more likely to reveal that they had been both physically and emotionally victimized. Victimization included several different types of behaviors, but it isn't specified how exactly "bullying prevention program" was defined. So it is hard to view this as evidence of failure, since we don't know anything about the programs that "failed." Also of note is the fact that these data were collected in 2005 and 2006—well before the federal and state governments mobilized their efforts against bullying.

More recently, Espelage and her colleagues reviewed 19 evaluations of bullying prevention programs and found that these efforts do OK with younger students (seventh grade and lower) but largely fail among students in high school: "Altogether, the present analysis suggests that we cannot yet confidently rely on anti-bullying programs for grades 8 and above."[8] David Finkelhor and his colleagues surveyed 3,391 5- to 17-year-olds and asked about their exposure to various violence prevention programs. They found that lower-quality programs, and those that targeted older youth, had less success in preventing participation in, and experience with, peer victimization.[9] Taken together, these academic articles paint a generally gloomy picture of the bullying prevention landscape.

SO WHERE DOES THIS LEAVE US?

Despite the depressing findings, I don't believe we should give up all hope. Sameer and I travel throughout the United States and speak with educators and students who are doing great things in their schools to prevent bullying and promote kindness and compassion. Our conversations with these people lead us to believe that some efforts are having the desired effect. The problem is that these initiatives have not been formally evaluated. In short, we are confident that effective actions are being taken in schools, but they need to be scrutinized, documented, and publicized.

In fact, Maria Ttofi and David Farrington (both from the University of Cambridge) conducted a more sophisticated analysis of 44 bullying prevention efforts (excluding programs that targeted violence or aggression generally) and uncovered some promising evidence: "school-based anti-bullying programs are effective: on average, bullying decreased by 20–23% and victimization decreased by 17–20%."[10] Ttofi and Farrington also go into specific detail about the elements of anti-bullying programs that seem to be the most effective (e.g., parent training, playground supervision, classroom management). Finkelhor and his colleagues agreed that there were some bright spots in the research: "Peer victimization rates and bullying perpetration rates in the past year were lower for the younger children (ages 5–9) who had been exposed to higher quality programs in their lifetime."[11] Higher-quality programs included "multi-day presentations, practice opportunities, information to take home, and [a] meeting for parents."[12]

> We are confident that effective actions are being taken in schools, but they need to be scrutinized, documented, and publicized.

This brings us back to the lessons learned in our attempts to curb crime. Upon closer review of Martinson's article, readers will realize that he was saying not that nothing could work, *just that our efforts at rehabilitation weren't being adequately funded to expect much of a change.*[13] The more things change, the more they stay the same. We still provide far too little funding to bullying prevention initiatives to help them do what they are intended to do. As with research on how to effectively prevent crime, Ttofi and Farrington find that "the intensity and duration of a program is directly linked to its effectiveness."[14] We can't spend just a few minutes once a year talking with students about bullying and expect it to be a long-term solution to this pernicious problem. A complicated social problem demands a comprehensive solution.

And there's also emerging evidence that bullying behaviors are decreasing (or at least not significantly increasing).[15] Recently released data from the National Crime Victimization Survey's School Crime Supplement shows that the percentage of students who said they were bullied in 2013 declined to 21.8% (from an average of 29.3% in the four previous biennial studies conducted between 2005 and 2011).[16] Cyberbullying rates also dropped in the most recent survey (from 9% in 2011 to 6.7% in 2013). It's still too early to tell if this is the beginning of a trend, or even if the numbers obtained are representative of an actual decrease in bullying behaviors across the United States. Other national sources of data don't depict similar decreases. The Youth Risk Behavior Surveillance System data, for example, found that 19.6% of students were bullied in 2013, compared to 20.1% in 2011.[17]

All of this said, I think it is safe to conclude that some programs work for some students in some schools under some circumstances. In short, *something works*. The bottom line is that we need to (1) identify promising programs (with meaningful intensity and duration), (2) fully fund these programs so they can do what they were designed to do, and (3) carefully evaluate the effectiveness of these programs. Armed with this information, legislators and policy makers can work with local school districts to promote best practices in bullying prevention. Only then will we begin to see sustainable reductions in problem behaviors.

QUESTIONS FOR REFLECTION

What works to prevent bullying in your school? Have you spoken to colleagues at other schools in your area about what they are doing to prevent bullying? How can we better promote positive initiatives to prevent bullying?

19

BULLYING ASSEMBLY PROGRAMS

What Schools Need to Know

Sameer Hinduja

Schools have been organizing assemblies to address bullying, substance abuse, and a variety of other student issues for as long as I can remember. I definitely recall sitting through them during middle school in particular, and—unfortunately—tuning out because I just didn't feel like I could connect with the speaker. When it came to the assemblies about bullying, I thought to myself, "Yes, we all realize that it's wrong to be mean to others, but nothing really is going to change at my school, so why even bother trying to make a difference?" I admit that was quite a defeatist mentality, but I'll blame it in large part on my disillusioned, angst-ridden adolescent self.

That said, I also remember more inspirational speakers who gave presentations at my schools, and while they weren't at all about bullying, I did find them compelling, hopeful, motivating, and even instructive. I didn't feel like I was being preached or lectured to, and that showed me I *could* be reached—it just really seemed to depend on the quality of the content, the tone of the message, the level at which I was spoken to, and the relatability

Assembly programs have value, but their selection and implementation require significant consideration and forethought.

of what was conveyed. The bottom line is that assembly programs have value, but their selection and implementation require significant consideration and forethought.

THE ASSEMBLY AS A BULLYING SOLUTION

Because school administrators know that bullying and cyberbullying are a problem on their campuses and want to do *something* about it, scheduling an assembly is often the very first idea that comes to their minds. It makes sense, because assemblies seem to be a relatively easy-to-implement solution. Typically, a school has a budget, and the administrators (or staff members) find a speaker, schedule the day and time, and bring the speaker in to do his or her thing in the auditorium, gymnasium, or cafeteria. This takes a lot less time and effort than what would be ideally implemented to make a true difference, but at least it is something.

To be sure, a *ton* of options are available for schools in this space. Just do a Google search for "bullying assembly" and you'll find pages and pages of potential speakers, many of whom are self-described "experts" (perhaps they are—I have no idea). Many educators also receive unsolicited e-mails from speakers, encouraging them to check out their websites and skill sets, and consider hiring them to talk to their students. The speakers' websites describe what makes their particular talks engaging, interactive, and motivating, and most provide testimonials highlighting the benefit their assemblies can provide to the school and attendant students. All of this is good. Really good. There is definitely a need to reach students with a gripping and powerful message that cultivates empathy, induces intentional kindness and respect toward their peers, and equips them to know exactly what to do if they—or someone they know—is being targeted. And there is definitely a need for *many* speakers to be out there doing their part to help. However, I want to make three points to help inform your implementation.

ASSEMBLIES MUST BE USED AS A SINGLE PIECE OF A MUCH BROADER EFFORT

While a bullying assembly does have some value, we cannot emphasize strongly enough that a "one and done" strategy will fall short and ring painfully hollow in time—even if it is the most heartrending or entertaining or memorable or impressive or convincing talk your students have ever heard.

They need more. Bullying prevention initiatives in schools can have assemblies as *part* of their programming, but according to the research, they need more substantive characteristics such as information sent home to parents, requests for parents to attend meetings (so as to get them on board to help educators with the message), instructive role-playing scenarios in the classroom, and efforts that last more than one day.[18] Schools need more than a flash-in-the-pan event, even if it is really good. The speaker's efforts can have great value as a launching pad from which other initiatives can take off. These can include a comprehensive anti-bullying *curriculum*; peer-to-peer *programming*, specifically training faculty and staff on how to teach digital civility and handle problems that arise; modules on socioemotional learning, stress management, and conflict resolution; social norming[19]; and building a positive school climate.[20]

CONSIDER THE IMPACT OF THE SPECIFIC CONTENT

A school's good intentions to impact, influence, and inspire its student body may backfire if the speaker or organization is not carefully vetted, and if the message is not carefully designed—with every word measured and every aspect planned and prepped for. For example, in 2014, one school district had significant reputational fallout in the community because it brought in a speaker whose interactive exercises may have contributed to excessive vulnerability (and even emotional and psychological pain) by students, and consequently further targeting by those who bully. At least one school district has been sued for indirectly contributing to a teen suicide by hiring a speaker who gave a presentation that may have planted ideas of self-harm as a viable option out of the pain one is experiencing.[21]

TAKE THE TIME TO FIND A GREAT SPEAKER TO OPTIMIZE CHANCES FOR SUCCESS

Schools interested in bringing out speakers to conduct student assemblies must demonstrate due diligence and do their background research. This is one of the primary ways to find out if the speakers are relatable and uplifting, and have great content that focuses on the positive, provides real solutions, and can lead to specific follow-up by the school. We suggest that educators reach out to colleagues at other schools for specific recommendations. Feel free to even cold-call those you don't know but who work at schools similar to your own. Feel free to review testimonials, but also know that a speaker's testimonials may not paint a full picture. As such, we also recommend that you take the time to schedule a phone call with potential speakers so you can get to know their style, passion, convictions, content areas, and exactly how they will connect with your students.

QUESTIONS FOR REFLECTION

What factors do you consider when selecting assembly speakers to reach your youth? What other activities do you use throughout the school year to promote bullying prevention?

20

What the Best Bullying and Cyberbullying Assembly Speakers Do

Sameer Hinduja

In Chapter 19, I shared what I feel are the most important considerations for schools planning to host bullying assembly programs. I need to also take some time to share some insight on the speakers themselves. As you may know from your own experiences, fantastic ones are out there, but many leave a lot to be desired. Justin and I have given assemblies all across the United States (and occasionally abroad), and truly enjoy visiting and working with students, staff, and parents in this capacity. However, we simply cannot do presentations for everyone, as much as we would love to. As such, here are my thoughts on what the best bullying and cyberbullying assembly speakers do.

SPEAKERS NEED TO BE RELATABLE

You may have heard that you win or lose your audience in the first few minutes of your talk. That is a short amount of time, and a lot of pressure to grab and hold listeners' attention. Relatable speakers will deeply connect with the audience by demonstrating complete familiarity of, and appreciation for, the offline and online world of teens (but not in a way that seems contrived or fake). In addition, they must immediately engage students—not with scare tactics—but by clarifying at the onset *why what they have to say matters to the students' very lives*. How is their message different from all of the other anti-bullying messages the students have heard before? Ultimately, the speaker is on their side. This is usually conveyed differently for elementary, middle, and high schoolers, and is a critically important skill to master. If the presentation somehow betrays that the speaker (and, by extension, the school) just doesn't "get" kids and teens these days, and doesn't really understand *fully* what is going on, its impact will be greatly stunted.

SPEAKERS NEED TO BE UPLIFTING

The overall message, on its whole, should be hopeful and empowering. No one wants to be completely bummed out and depressed after listening to a speaker. That totally and completely drains away the audience's desire and motivation to try and make a difference. Yes, students need to understand the weight of pain, regret, and potential consequences that surround bullying and cyberbullying, but they cannot flourish and meaningfully contribute to a better peer and school environment under that burden. No one can. And no one will want to. Speakers must make sure the presentation is balanced, and leaves students feeling fired up and equipped to foster change.

SPEAKERS NEED TO FOCUS ON THE POSITIVE

Many adults are keen to focus on teen conflict, drama, harassment, and hate, and share those stories in an attempt to motivate youth to do the opposite instead. But we've found that those good intentions don't lead to the desired effect. Instead, they can come across as condescending and preachy. Being subjected to those stories makes teens feel that adults expect the worst of them, and that they need to be managed and controlled instead of trusted and empowered. Justin and I strongly believe that speakers must point out all of the *good* that teens are doing as they embrace social media and electronic communications, instead of emphasizing all of the ways in which students have screwed up. Speakers should try to inspire them by showing them examples of teens *just like them* who are making a difference by standing up for what's right. An increasing number of websites are sharing meaningful stories of teens (and adults) doing kind things! Check out our Words Wound movement, *The Huffington Post*'s Good News, Upworthy, One Good Thing, or A Platform for Good for ideas. Ideally, seeds will be planted in some of the youth.[22] Then, they hopefully will be motivated to replicate the ideas discussed, or come up with their own (specific to their skills and situations) and work to contribute to widespread change on their campus.

> Speakers must point out all of the *good* that teens are doing as they embrace social media and electronic communications, instead of emphasizing all of the ways in which students have screwed up.

SPEAKERS NEED TO HAVE GREAT CONTENT

The data, stories, and examples speakers share must align with and reflect what the students have been observing and experiencing on their own, or else their message will be discredited and dismissed as irrelevant. The presentation should be interactive, fun, solemn at times (I mean, we are ultimately discussing a pretty serious topic here!), memorable, smooth, and somehow unique. It should also be updated with the latest research (when appropriate, don't bore the audience with bar charts!), trends, headlines, stories, and screenshots. Many speakers want to do this, but honestly never really get around to updating their presentations. This will not win over the audience or keep them locked into what is being shared. Speakers should remember that students have heard this message before, and their default reaction will be to tune out because of the way this topic has been browbeaten into them. This is why content is—and always will be—"king."

SPEAKERS SHOULD INCLUDE SOLUTIONS

Students want to know whom they can trust and confide in if they are being mistreated. They want to know how to really, truly get someone to stop being mean, how to anonymously report problems, and how to block mean people on specific networks or apps. They want clear direction as to how to intervene so that it doesn't backfire on them, and how best to help others in a way that is safe for them as well.[23] They need clear, specific strategies that are age-appropriate and will actually work. At the same time, schools need to know that a good number of presentations are *high on inciting emotional responses* but *low on solutions*. Just make sure you identify your goals at the outset so you are not left feeling like something is missing after the presentation(s).

SPEAKERS SHOULD HAVE A PLAN FOR FOLLOW-UP

Speakers should have books, materials, activities, or resources—*something* they can distribute to the school so that faculty and staff can debrief with the students and thereby continue the conversation after the assembly (and, ideally, on a regular basis throughout the year). The resources should clearly mirror the messages conveyed in the assembly so that everything builds on itself. If the speaker doesn't have content to share, he or she should be able to recommend the best out there. This simply demonstrates that the speaker knows the proverbial lay of the land, and has taken the time to figure out what can help the school on a long-term basis with its bullying prevention goals.

Ultimately, a great speaker with great content makes for a great presentation. I know that sounds intuitive, which is why I wanted to drill down into the essential components to show you what matters the most. I hope the preceding helps those on the front lines working hard to raise awareness on this incredibly important issue. If we are spending our lives (and the time, attention, and resources of schools) trying to communicate a truly transformative message, we must give it our best—and do it right.

QUESTIONS FOR REFLECTION

What is your experience with speakers who have come to talk to your students? Has their message, tone, and advice been in line with the points presented above? What have the best and worst speakers at your school done over the years?

21

Student Advisory Boards Can Inform Bullying Policies and Prevention

Sameer Hinduja

Whenever I visit schools to give a cyberbullying assembly or presentation to parents in the community, I am also typically asked to sit down and chat with the administrators about the policies and programs they have in place. Here, they let me know what they have been doing to identify, address, and prevent teen technology misuse, and then detail some of the struggles that they have faced—like how to talk about sexting without sounding irrelevant, how to develop penalties for rule breaking that can be consistently enforced and supported by all, and how to strategically encourage kindness and peer respect in a compelling way. Apart from sharing with them evolving best practices, I encourage them to invite *students* to the table when determining what can and should be done.

STUDENTS SHOULD ALWAYS FEEL THAT THEY HAVE A VOICE AT SCHOOL

Having a voice at school means that students' input on school activities, curriculum, teaching styles, field trips, behavioral issues on campus, and other matters is valued and taken into consideration. I strongly believe that the relevant decision makers at each school should regularly meet with student leaders or even consider convening a "Student Advisory Board" composed of teens who want to get involved in the governance of their school. In this setting, administrators should solicit and take student perspectives into account when figuring out strategies and solutions, and continually welcome students' thoughts and input on these matters.

STUDENTS KNOW—BETTER THAN ANYONE ELSE—WHAT DEVICES, PROGRAMS, OR SITES ARE BEING EMBRACED AND EXPLOITED BY THEIR PEER GROUP

Students can clue you in to the latest popular social media apps that have gained a lot of traction on campus, the newest online gaming communities, and the hottest technology tools (along with their capabilities). They can then inform you about some of the problems they have seen online among their friends, such as cyberbullying, sexting, anonymous threats, and major digital reputation issues. It is crucial to create a nonjudgmental and safe environment in which you regularly invite both older and younger student leaders to candidly provide feedback on the tech-related misbehaviors they see and hear about (or even participate in).

GET THE STUDENTS' "INSIDER" PERSPECTIVE

Getting the students' insider perspective will allow you to better determine the comprehensiveness of your policy, its deterrent value among students (if any), how consistently it is enforced, and whether it is respected. Because the majority of students use technology safely and responsibly—and are often afforded certain device privileges on campus—they won't want that access taken away from them. Therefore, it is in their best interest to *help* adults in identifying problem areas and getting them resolved so that the misbehavior of one or two students doesn't ruin it for everyone else.

As an added benefit, students who are involved in reviewing the bullying policies cannot say that they "don't know" that their bullying behavior is wrong, and using students to help define the behaviors (and even possible penalties for breaking the rules) will ensure that the policies are up to date and applicable to contemporary concerns. Plus, *if students are a part of policy development, they have a stake in the successful implementation of policies.* When new or revised policies are developed, students can help get the word out. For example, the Student Advisory Board could go into individual classes for a few minutes to talk about the purpose of the new policies, share it over the morning or afternoon announcements, or write about it for the school paper, website, or yearbook. *The more you educate students about potential issues and concerns, the more willing they are to take ownership of reasonable policies to prevent the misuse of technology.*

It is also a good idea to give youth an opportunity to offer constructive criticism on the wording of your formal rules, the informal and formal penalties tied to various transgressions, and the curricula and related programming you have in

> If students are a part of policy development, they have a stake in the successful implementation of policies.

place (or are considering). Allow students to articulate their thoughts and suggestions about what *they* believe will work to change prevailing mentalities across campus, and meaningfully promote a school climate that is all about appropriate and responsible behaviors (at school and online). Truly, they will let you know what they think is "lame" and what they think will actually succeed.

LISTEN TO STUDENTS

The last thing you want to do is waste time, effort, and resources on a creative initiative that the adults think is a fantastic idea but ends up completely and utterly failing among students. To be honest, that will do more bad than good by reaffirming student suspicion that the school is oblivious and completely out of the loop. Since teens are fully immersed in all things technological and social, it is crucial to enlist their help in determining how best the school can equip the student body with the skills and knowledge to be great digital citizens, how best to pitch responsible online behavior as "cool" and "what we do around here," and how best to get everyone on board.

QUESTIONS FOR REFLECTION

Do you have a formal mechanism for the voices of students to be heard, and consequently to inform your policies and procedures? How can you increasingly encourage youth to be the "eyes and ears" on campus to clue you in to what will work best (and what will fail) when it comes to bullying and cyberbullying prevention?

22

DETERRING TEEN BULLYING

Dos and Don'ts

Justin W. Patchin

There's been a lot of interest lately in passing new bullying and cyberbullying laws.[24] The pressure to pursue these provisions seems to come from the idea that the threat of harsher penalties will deter teens from bullying others. But will it? Deterrence theory is a very popular philosophy within the criminal justice system, and as such serves as the basis for many policies (e.g., mandatory sentences, "three strikes" laws).[25] The premise is simple: Humans are rational beings who weigh the costs and benefits of any behavior and ultimately act in a way that maximizes pleasure and minimizes pain. Rational people are therefore more likely to refrain from deviance when the costs (severe punishment) are increased.

The problem with this perspective is that adolescent brains haven't yet fully developed to the point where we can assume rationality in the face of unknown or unlikely consequences.[26] Moreover, we often focus too much on formal punishment as a means to compel compliance instead of recognizing other powerful forces that may be even more effective.[27] So what can be done to deter teens from bullying others? Below I offer some basic bullying deterrence dos and don'ts.

DETERRENCE DON'TS

Don't increase formal sanctions. As noted above, a lot of people have been pushing for increased criminal penalties to be leveled against those who participate in bullying. Bills have been passed or proposed in most states even while legislation has been languishing at the federal level since 2009.[28] New laws that clarify and support the roles of educators in responding to bullying are helpful, but those that seek to further criminalize are not likely to be effective at preventing the behaviors.

Based on all that we have learned working with teens, it is unlikely that new criminal laws will result in more teens being deterred from engaging in bullying. Those who were dissuaded before will still be, but the added threat of increased legal punishment isn't likely to prevent additional people from participating. The problem is that most teens (and many adults, for that matter) simply don't stop to consider the possible costs (especially the possible criminal consequences) prior to participating in a behavior.[29] They are usually absorbed in the moment and aren't thinking about what could happen if they are caught. Plus, the odds are good that they won't be caught (or significantly punished).

> Most teens simply don't stop to consider the possible costs (especially the possible criminal consequences) prior to participating in a behavior.

Don't enact zero-tolerance policies. Zero-tolerance policies require school administrators to apply a specific, generally severe sanction (often suspension or even expulsion) to a student who is found to have participated in some proscribed behavior. These policies were most often originally focused on curbing weapon and drug possession at school, but in recent years, they have been expanded to include other forms of violence and bullying. Don't get me wrong—"zero tolerance" is a fine idea in theory. Educators do want to clearly communicate that they have zero tolerance for weapons or drugs or bullying in their schools and that those who violate this standard are certain to be punished. The problem is that these policies—by definition—do not allow educators to use their discretion to handle situations outside the letter of the policy. Bullying is largely a relationship problem, and educators, working with parents, need to use their knowledge of the situation to apply a reasonable sanction that is more uniquely designed to address the particular problem at hand. One-size-fits-all responses frequently fall short in issues involving teens.[30]

Don't utilize public shaming. Shame is a powerful force that can be used to encourage conformity and compliance. But when misused, it can result in the exact opposite response. Historically, societies have used shame to induce guilt among those who behave in ways that are counter to societal norms.[31] Shaming can also have the unintended side effect of severing the emotional bond between the person(s) doing the shaming and the one being shamed.

Australian criminologist John Braithwaite argues that there are two types of shaming: disintegrative (or stigmatizing) and reintegrative.[32] Disintegrative shaming results when society identifies a person as deviant, and figuratively (or even literally) expels that person from the conforming group. Reintegrative shaming occurs when society condemns the *behavior*, but not the *person*. In this case, we avoid labeling someone "a bully" but instead refer to the specific bullying behaviors that need to stop. It is not the child we are convicting, but his or her behavior. Even when done with the best intentions in mind, public shaming is too risky when applied to adolescents whose self-esteem is generally fragile and underdeveloped.[33]

There have been a number of recent examples of parents (or even educators) publicly shaming their kids to send them (and others) a message about the wrongfulness of their behavior. North Carolina parent Tommy Jordan made an 8-minute YouTube video condemning his 15-year-old daughter for misbehavior that culminated in him shooting the daughter's laptop with nine hollow-point bullets.[34] Denise Abbott is an Ohio mother who punished her 13-year-old daughter for being disrespectful by posting a picture of her with an "X" across her mouth with the caption: "I do not know how to keep my mouth shut. I am no longer allowed on Facebook or my phone. Please ask me why."[35]

This approach is misplaced. In my view, parents who publicly shame their kids do so primarily because they feel publicly humiliated by the actions of their children and so need to prove that they are "good" parents by punishing their children in a public way. While this might seem like a creative method to address the behavior, I believe it can do more harm than good. The importance of the parent–child emotional bond cannot be overstressed, and permanent damage can be done. Praise publicly; punish privately.

Canadian cyberbullying educator and speaker Lissa Albert has also raised the question, if the behavior does change, is it because the child has

> Public shaming is too risky when applied to adolescents whose self-esteem is generally fragile and underdeveloped. Praise publicly; punish privately.

learned a lesson, or because the child has been severely intimidated by his or her public shaming that called further attention to his or her rule breaking?[36] The goal of discipline should not be to instill fear of the punishment; it should be to bring about a change in behavior as a result of understanding why the behavior needs changing. In addition, these examples provide a dangerous precedent for what could be considered *bullying on the part of parents toward their own children*. These are the very people who are supposed to be *protecting* their kids from the world, not exposing and humiliating them.

DETERRENCE DOS

Do give students a stake in conformity. The threat of punishment only works if people have something of value in their life that they would risk losing if punished. For example, earning a bad grade only hurts if a student cares about good grades or is aiming for college or a scholarship. After-school detention is most powerful when students have something else they really like to do after school that they would miss out on (such as an extra-curricular activity or hanging out with friends). Taking this a step further, if a man is unemployed, homeless, and broke, the threat of brief incarceration isn't really enough to stop him from misbehaving. At least in jail he will be given a bed to sleep on and a meal to eat. As Bob Dylan famously sang, "When you ain't got nothing, you got nothing to lose." The best thing we can do for students to deter them from mistreating others is to get them involved in positive, socially connected activities that they really enjoy so that the threat of school sanction or parental punishment holds weight.

Moreover, the punishment doesn't necessarily have to be particularly serious to have an effect. For instance, at least as of right now, I have a perfectly clean driving record. I have never been pulled over for any moving violation in over two decades of driving [*knock on wood*]. As much as the threat of receiving a modest monetary fine deters me from speeding, my desire to keep my record unblemished is an even stronger incentive, at least for me.

Do connect and interact. Another reason many people refrain from misbehavior is that they don't want to disappoint the people in their lives whom they care about. Prevention is all about relationships. Inasmuch as many teens are not deterred by the threat of formal punishment, they *are* dissuaded from participation in behaviors that they know their friends, parents, or other valued adults would frown on.[37] When teens are emotionally attached or socially bonded to others, they internalize their norms and values and do not want to disappoint these people by behaving in a way that is contradictory to those principles.

The concept of *virtual supervision* demonstrates that kids will behave in ways that are consistent with the behavior of adults they value and respect, even when those valued others are not directly supervising them.[38] For example, if I really value my relationship with my mom, and I know that she would be disappointed in me if she knew that I bullied someone, then I am less likely to bully others. This is true even in situations where she is not present, because I am considering how my mom might feel if she found out about my behavior (and my mom *always* finds out). Of course, this only works if I have a really great relationship with my mom and don't want to damage that relationship by disappointing her. So the key here is developing strong relationships between adults and kids.

This powerful effect can also impact others who work with young people (educators, religious leaders, and law enforcement officers, to name a few). As an example, one time when I was in high school, I drove my ATV

> When teens are emotionally attached or socially bonded to others, they internalize their norms and values and do not want to disappoint these people by behaving in a way that is contradictory to those principles.

across town to a community event. Several minutes after I got there, one of the local police officers arrived and immediately started chewing me out for driving too fast on the city streets. He was yelling at me, saying that after he saw me he went to my house and waited for me and was going to give me a speeding ticket! For the record, I really didn't think I was going that fast. Nonetheless, I was devastated. I was embarrassed and upset that I had disappointed him—not just because he was a police officer, or because he was threatening to give me a ticket, but because he had been my hockey coach the year prior and I had a great relationship with him. I felt terrible. In the end, he didn't give me a ticket, but from then on, I drove very slowly when navigating the city streets on my ATV.

It was a very powerful experience that others can learn from. Take the time to develop a positive relationship with your kids and students. For decades, we have known the power of spending just a bit of regular time with students (e.g., two minutes a day for ten days in a row).[39] Learn their names. Give them high-fives as they come off the bus. Show them that you care—because we know you do. It can make all the difference.

Do develop a positive school climate. A positive school climate stimulates and encourages respect, cooperation, trust, and a shared responsibility for the educational goals that exist in a school.[40] Here, educators, students, and everyone connected to the school take ownership of its mission and work together toward a shared vision. If a climate like this is established, everything else seems to fall into place. Research consistently demonstrates that the more positive the climate of the school is, the fewer problems there are with bullying (and cyberbullying).[41] A sense of collective concern is cultivated where students just seem to look out for each other more and believe that the adults in the school are genuinely there to help.

Since schools with better climates overall have fewer bullying incidents, a self-fulfilling prophecy emerges over time where eventually, *bullying just doesn't happen there.*[42] If it does, it is addressed and stopped immediately. Students see that and are less inclined to resort to bullying in cases of conflict.

CONCLUSION

Deterring negative behaviors in a society requires more than just passing a new law or cranking up the consequences in existing laws. Considerate understanding of the needs and desires of teens will help us to design a measured and informed response that is more likely to be effective. The simple fact is that some teens will not be deterred in their behaviors by the threat of any formal, criminal punishment, no matter how severe it may be. But these same youth can be prevented from bullying others if they have caring relationships with others or are involved in activities that they value.

QUESTIONS FOR REFLECTION

Can teens really be deterred from engaging in bullying? In your opinion, what works best to deter teens from participating in bullying? Can you think of any other "dos or don'ts" to add to this list?

23

Should Schools Monitor Students' Social Media Accounts?

Justin W. Patchin

I n recent years, there has been much discussion about whether it is appropriate for schools to actively monitor the social media activities of students. At the center of this debate is Glendale Unified School District, which is located in Southern California and has a middle and high school student population of about 14,000. In 2013, the district contracted with Geo Listening (a Hermosa Beach, California–based tech company founded in January of that year) to monitor and keep track of the various things its student body says, posts, shares, and does online (at a cost of $40,500 for the school year). As of the start of the 2015–2016 school year, a few other schools had publicly partnered with companies to monitor the behavior of students online.[43]

Geo Listening states that it actively looks for anything online that could threaten the safety and well-being of students in the district, including cyberbullying and threats of self-harm. These could be posts that are initiated from school, or not; using school-owned technology, or not. The technology also allows for the flagging and reporting of drug use or class cutting—or really anything publicly posted by a student that could be viewed as problematic to the school.

Sameer and I are contacted fairly regularly by tech companies that have developed a technological "solution" to cyberbullying that they are looking to market to schools. We've yet to be swept off our feet by any of these proposed solutions, and what Geo Listening is doing is similarly not very innovative or revolutionary. That said, the question remains: should schools be in the business of actively monitoring what their students are saying online?

PARENTAL MONITORING

Most people would agree that parents have a responsibility to keep tabs on what their kids are doing online. This is best accomplished, in my view, by actively participating in online activities with them and asking questions about what they are posting and who they are interacting with. Parents frequently ask me, though, whether it is a good idea to install tracking or monitoring software on their child's device(s) as a way to monitor. This is a tough issue. On the one hand, I am not in a position to tell anyone how to parent his or her kids. So when responding to this question, I simply explain the potential consequences of going this route. If parents choose to *surreptitiously* monitor the online activities of their offspring, eventually they *will* find something to confront their kids about. When they do, and the children find out that their parents have been spying on them, it will be extremely difficult to repair the harm done since finding the information required a clear violation of the existing trust relationship.

In general, if parents think it is necessary to take such a step, I advise them to make their kids aware of it. Parents should tell their children why they are installing the software and explain that the primary goal is to protect them. Finally, parents should use this as an opportunity to encourage responsible use by informing their children that as they demonstrate safe and appropriate behaviors online over time, they will gradually earn more privacy. This can be a very effective strategy for early Internet users who are still learning how to safely navigate social media and the web. A concern I have is that some parents may fall into a false sense of security when they hear that the school is paying someone to watch over what their kids are doing online, and therefore not take the time to do it themselves.

The reality, of course, is that if children want to circumvent tracking and monitoring software, it is pretty easy to do. They will go online at a friend's house using a borrowed device, or log on from another location, such as McDonald's or the local public library. I have even had two separate principals in different schools tell me that an 18-year-old senior had picked up a

TracFone or other pay-as-you-go device from Walmart to give to his younger girlfriend, whose mom and dad didn't even know that she had it. The point is, if you push too hard, teens will go underground, which will make it even more difficult to keep up. Finally, research has cast doubt on the effectiveness of monitoring and blocking software in preventing experiences with cyberbullying.[44] It simply is not *the* solution that parents are often looking for (and unfortunately one just doesn't exist).

PRIVACY CONCERNS

Some argue that schools monitoring social media amounts to a violation of students' privacy.[45] I am not particularly convinced of that. Most students I speak with are savvy enough to realize that what they post in public spaces online is open for anyone to see. And they know that schools are looking. Counselors, principals, and school resource officers have been perusing profiles for years. The only thing new about this is that a school is contracting with a third party to do the watching.

Most students say that they have their Facebook accounts set to private.[46] Indeed, in our early research into the social media behaviors of students on Myspace (remember that site?), we found that in 2006 less than 40% of students had set their profiles to private.[47] By 2009, 85% of active users had their profiles restricted. And this was not a survey of students where we asked them to report what they were doing. We randomly selected profiles to carefully review to see how much information was publicly visible. So very early on—over seven years ago—students recognized the need to avoid having their profiles open for the whole world to see. In addition, more and more teens are moving to ephemeral communication apps like Snapchat that make it more difficult to watch over and track what they are saying.

SCHOOL CULTURE IS WHAT MATTERS MOST

From my perspective, schools (along with parents, of course) do have an obligation to keep track of what students are doing online. I don't feel, however, that schools should need to go on fishing expeditions where they scour the web and social media for inappropriate behaviors. In a perfect world, paying a company to watch over the online interactions of students wouldn't be necessary. I feel that schools should spend those resources to help develop a culture where everyone looks out for everyone else, and where if something of concern arises, *someone* will step up and take appropriate action.[48] Most of the time, when there is a threat to cause harm—either to oneself or to others—someone sees or hears about it. What do students do at that moment? Are they empowered to take action themselves? Do they feel comfortable talking with an adult at school about what they witnessed or heard about? Do they feel that telling an adult at school or at home will resolve the situation?

> Schools should work to develop a culture where everyone looks out for everyone else, and where if something of concern arises, *someone* will step up and take appropriate action.

An added benefit is that, by encouraging and empowering students to come forward with concerns, schools have many more people on the lookout for trouble and are able to access much more potentially problematic information since even private profiles (not accessible to a third-party monitoring company) are visible to at least some students.

Consider this contradiction: When you ask students what they should do if they are being cyberbullied, or if they see it happen, more often than not, they will respond with "Tell an adult." Yet, when you ask them if telling an adult will help, they often say no! According to the Youth Voice Project, a survey of nearly 12,000 students from 12 different U.S. states conducted by Stan Davis and Charisse Nixon, only about one-third of the students who were significantly impacted by bullying said that telling an adult made things better (29% said it made things worse!).[49] So perhaps the main problem isn't so much that schools need to do a better job of paying attention to what is going on online, but instead they need to do a better job thinking about how best to respond. If schools are able to respond to bullying and cyberbullying in a way that quickly stops the harassment without further harming or humiliating any of the parties involved, then students will feel much more comfortable going to the adults at school for help when problems arise in the future. And the word will spread, encouraging others to also do so. As it is, many students are afraid that the school, or their parents, will just make things worse, and so they often choose instead to suffer silently or mind their own business if they see others targeted.

So the more important question for me is what do the educators do with the information once they receive it? The company sends the school district a daily report of online chatter that might be important to investigate further. Who is responsible for investigating? Who decides whether something is serious enough to warrant additional scrutiny? Are schools taking on additional liability by actively patrolling the Internet for problems? What if there is a threat that the school should have seen but didn't? What if a school is made aware of a threat but doesn't act quickly enough? There are so many unanswered questions.

JUSTIFIABLE USE OF RESOURCES?

Another issue is whether this is a good use of school resources. Where I live in Wisconsin, $40,000 could be used to hire an additional school counselor, at least part-time. At a time when school budgets are shrinking and support staff are routinely being cut, are schools trying to cut corners by relying on a technological solution to a social problem? And are they right for doing so? Some schools might use this service as a way to avoid paying for much more comprehensive and effective strategies to prevent online and offline bullying before it happens (e.g., social emotional learning programming). Monitor, respond, repeat. It is always best, of course, to prevent these things from happening in the first place, but prevention often costs more up front (even though in the long run it is always much less expensive).

The weight of public opinion seems to be in support of schools paying others to monitor their students online. I'm still not convinced. It makes sense that schools want to be made aware of potentially problematic situations developing on social media (and the earlier the better). But it remains to be seen whether this tactic will be effective. As a researcher, I would love to evaluate this program. This could make for a valuable research project if a school district would randomly assign schools to participate in this and then follow up to see if there are any changes in student perceptions or behaviors. It would also be helpful to know, for example, how many suicides really can be prevented using something like this. Glendale and Geo Listening claim that at least one suicide was thwarted in their pilot test of this last year, but it is uncertain whether someone at the school came across the information and reported it without the aid of the service.

QUESTIONS FOR REFLECTION

Does your school formally monitor the online activities of students? Do you think it is a good idea for schools to contract with third-party vendors to provide this service? What benefits do you see? Are there any concerns not addressed in this chapter?

24

Addressing Discrimination to Prevent Bullying

Sameer Hinduja

W e believe that schools across the United States should be sacred institutions for learning, where students feel secure and free to focus and interact without worry or fear. We can't do much about some of the things they worry and are fearful about, but we definitely can do a lot about harassment, hate, bullying, and threats of harm or violence. Educators have so much to deal with on their weekly agendas, but this has to take precedent over other priorities. We've told you that around 20% of youth are cyberbullied during their lives.[50] Well, we don't want 20% of the next generation dealing with some or all of the fallout we've identified as consequences and outcomes for those victimized (lower self-esteem, negative emotions, emotional and psychological issues, delinquency and crime, and suicidal thoughts/attempts).[51]

Since you're reading this book, it's likely that you are the type of person who will step in when you see overt bullying or cyberbullying, and address it in some form or fashion. *Thank you*. That needs to happen every time, and we are encouraged to see increasing numbers of school personnel across the nation step up to the proverbial plate on this issue. But what we'd like to see more of is a conscious effort to train and empower educators (administrators, counselors, teachers, coaches, and support staff) to preempt bullying and cyberbullying by identifying and correcting some of their contributive elements. For example, incidents of hate and harassment are often rooted in discrimination, so we believe that meaningful progress can be made by focusing in on that particular element. Doing so may prevent the manifestation of more serious conflicts and outcomes.

School personnel are morally and legally obligated to provide a safe educational environment for all students—one that is free from discrimination.[52] Title IX of the Education Amendments of 1972 requires schools to prevent and address sexual harassment and sex discrimination, and its interpretation has been broadened in the decades since its passage.[53] It is safe to say that any form of discrimination occurring on campus that undermines a child's ability to feel safe and concentrate on learning must be addressed if it is made known to school officials. Not only is addressing such behavior mandated by law, but not dealing with it can lead to claims of negligence and financial liability (as well as reputational damage) if harm to a student occurs based on discrimination.[54]

> School personnel are morally and legally obligated to provide a safe educational environment for all students—one that is free from discrimination.

We believe that all forms of peer harassment—on a fundamental level—involve some type of *discrimination*. This could be discrimination based on how someone looks, dresses, acts, speaks, or simply "is." Youth can take the smallest difference and magnify it to cause drama, to build themselves up while tearing another down, or to indulge an impulse—in other words, just because they feel like it.

A quick story for you—and hopefully you can see the link. . . . When we were in school, we couldn't wear T-shirts with inappropriate slogans or depictions. Occasionally, we heard of a student being sent to the principal's office and forced to wear the shirt inside out or made to wait until his parents brought another shirt to wear for the rest of the day. This might not seem like that big a deal, but there is logic behind these rules and actions. First, inappropriate content on T-shirts compromises the positive, safe, wholesome atmosphere that schools strive to provide. That might sound idealistic, but part of any school's mandate is to create and maintain a learning environment that is respectful, inclusive, and supportive so that *all* students can have *every* opportunity to succeed.[55]

Second, such shirts can be offensive and discriminatory to other students and staff at school and therefore infringe on their civil rights. As an example, in 2008 the U.S. Court of Appeals upheld a Tennessee school's decision to punish a student for wearing a Confederate flag T-shirt, agreeing with school administrators that the shirts would cause a substantial disruption among students and staff on campus.[56] Here, concerns of school safety amid a climate of racial unrest in the community and on campus contributed to the ruling (demonstrating the importance of always taking into account the surrounding context of every situation).

Third, they unnecessarily attract negative attention and thereby distract students from learning. Schools, then, can respond to problematic content— or the behavior that creates such content—if its effects are detrimental to their purpose and goals (such as constructing and maintaining a safe school environment!). Such content and behavior start with *inappropriate clothing*, *inappropriate words*, and *inappropriate actions* (like shaming, excluding, and ostracizing) and, if not dealt with, can subsequently lead to more severe forms of interpersonal harm.

Educators and other youth-serving professionals need to remember that they have more authority than they think as it relates to these sorts of issues.[57] We encourage you to take the time to address even the most subtle forms of discrimination you see. Set a hard-and-fast line, and create a climate among everyone at school (adults and teens) demonstrating that "we" are all about inclusivity, mutual respect, kindness, and "bro" moves.[58] Call it out when you see it, and end it one-on-one with the offending student or in front of everyone (if it was an accident or joke that simply wasn't thought through and can serve as a teachable moment). The hope is that even though you can't see or measure its value in the present, doing so will cut down on the frequency and scope of bullying and cyberbullying among your students in the future.

QUESTIONS FOR REFLECTION

In what specific ways have you worked to cultivate an environment that prioritizes inclusivity, embraces diversity, and promotes peer respect across all possible dividing lines? How are you enlisting youth to help you maintain this environment? How have other faculty and staff helped you? Finally, is there a way that you can get parents on board to reinforce this message?

25

Ideas to Make Kindness Go Viral

Sameer Hinduja

One of the main points that Justin and I have been emphasizing in our school trainings and presentations is that we don't just want students to *not* do the wrong thing (i.e., not engage in bullying and cyberbullying). Rather, we want them to actively do the right thing (i.e., do their part in contributing to a kinder, better climate on their school campus and in their community). If I were still a student, I wouldn't want to attend a school where the kids aren't mean to each other but they are also not nice to each other. Instead, they just keep their heads down, mind their own business, and live their own lives in a very insular and self-focused way. That doesn't get me excited or hopeful at all about my middle school or high school life, and it makes me feel like everyone just needs to "gut it out" in survival mode and wish for better days on the other side of it.

I want to go to a school where my fellow classmates and peers are invested in building and maintaining an environment marked by care, compassion, and mutual respect. Then I'd be stoked to get there in the morning and be a part of something healthy and vibrant—something that is thriving.

> We don't just want kids and teens to *not* do the wrong thing. Rather, we want them to actively do the right thing.

Based on our experiences working with tens of thousands of youth, I feel like they want that—they just don't know how to make it happen, and happen in a way that gains traction and succeeds, instead of failing and appearing lame or uncool. So the adults in their life need to teach them, inspire them, and help them along. To be sure, sometimes educators naively expect kids to know and apply the Golden Rule in all their interactions from early childhood. However, without intentional efforts to instruct and cultivate kindness, your students are simply not going to be others-focused by default.

Interestingly, research now shows that people who learn about, and practice demonstrating, compassion and empathy toward others are more likely to establish long-term patterns of positive behavior. Richard Davidson at the University of Wisconsin in Madison and his colleagues have been studying the ways that compassionate behavior actually changes the brain. They found that "participants who learned compassion were more generous" and that "greater generosity . . . was associated with changes in the brain's response to human suffering in regions involved in empathy and increasing positive emotions."[59] In short, encouraging kids and teens to be kind and caring can result in neurological changes that may lead to expanded and consistent kindness and compassion toward others.

With all of this in mind, we'd like to provide you with some specific ways you can encourage and equip the youth in your life to combat bullying and cyberbullying by making it cool to care about others—both offline and online.

SET UP A SOCIAL MEDIA COMPLIMENTS PAGE

Most teens have a profile on one or more social networking platforms and are very comfortable navigating these environments. Perhaps you can encourage students to set up a separate account for the purpose of dishing out anonymous accolades to their classmates. This idea was made famous by Kevin Curwick's @OsseoNiceThings Twitter feed and Jeremiah Anthony's "West High Bros" Facebook compliments page and @WestHighBros Twitter feed. Now dozens of social media accounts have been set up by teens for the purpose of encouraging and praising their peers.

PARTICIPATE IN RANDOM ACTS OF KINDNESS

More and more individuals in all walks of life are realizing that it's actually really cool to be kind. It's even cooler when kindness is dished out anonymously and unexpectedly. Encourage your students or children to engage in random acts of kindness in their school or broader community. Search online for examples of young people being kind to others to give them inspiration. Dozens of videos and even a Twitter hashtag (#RandomActofKindness) can direct you to ideas as well.

CREATE A PUBLIC SERVICE ANNOUNCEMENT

Many teens have great ideas for promoting positivity that they would love to share with others. Give them creative freedom to script out and record a short video with the simple purpose of encouraging others to be kind. They can interview their classmates or "famous" people in their school or community (like the principal or mayor). Leave up to them how to approach the activity—they'll surprise you and hopefully come up with something really compelling! Then you can upload it to YouTube, your school's web page, or social media accounts, and otherwise use it as a teaching tool to reach so many others!

MAKE POSTERS

A simple activity that kids of all ages can tackle is to design inspirational posters that can be plastered on walls around the school. It doesn't take much artistic talent to inspire others to be kind with drawings or creative slogans. Teachers can work with a particular class or a specific subset of students to produce posters that can be covertly placed all over the school on Friday afternoon or over the weekend. The rest of the student body will return on Monday and be totally inspired by what they see all around them.

In closing, remember that promoting kindness doesn't have to be a big production. The best ideas are often among the simplest. Working together, parents, teachers, and teens can make tremendous strides toward combating cruelty in all its forms during each new school year. Hopefully, as you share these ideas and stories of kindness, your teens will feel compelled to write their own, and thereby leave a positive mark in their school, community, and beyond.

QUESTIONS FOR REFLECTION

Which ideas—of those above—do you believe will gain the most traction among your student body? Do any others come to mind that can promote positivity? How can you informally marshal the role of peer pressure in inducing participation in more kindness initiatives?

26

Anti-Bullying Youth Rally at Schools

Sameer Hinduja

Pep rallies for middle and high school athletic teams have been going on for decades, and are always great ways to get fired up about the sports season or the next big game. They serve multiple purposes, all of which are quite important. For one, they really heighten school spirit—and if I am a student, I want to be excited about my school and believe in its chance and ability for success and victory. Second, it's related to our identity, and our desire to be part of something bigger than ourselves. In this case, if you are a student, you belong to a group—whether you are the Knights, the Fighting Owls, the Blugolds, or the Spartans. You're not alone; you are supporting something and working toward something together, with your peers—people you know and hopefully care about. Third, pep rallies break up the monotony of the school routine, and provide a fun, energetic, and inspiring outlet for everyone. This matters; students need this on a regular basis.

Some schools are starting to hold pep rallies to promote academic success (instead of only athletic success), and figure out a creative way to recognize those on the Dean's List, on the Honor Roll, or otherwise doing awesome things toward their academic goals or for the betterment of the community. Well, we are also starting to see a trend where some schools—as spearheaded by motivated and passionate teens—decide to put on an anti-bullying pep rally. Now, this is a bit tricky because everyone will be like, "Why are we being called into the gymnasium [or auditorium]?" "What is going on here?" "Man, I hope this doesn't suck!" And so it will be up to interested students and faculty/staff to come up with a really enjoyable, meaningful experience where you do each of the following:

1. Talk about how bullying, drama, and other conflicts are specifically affecting your school and the students in it (be real, be honest, and speak from the heart!)

2. Share about how, in order for everyone to have a great school year, it has got to stop

3. Tie it into the fact that everyone is a Greyhound, a Dolphin, or a Tiger (etc.), and how being a part of this group means that everyone should act in a certain way and not be a jerk toward others (there is a responsibility to do the right thing, and most *are* doing the right thing, but everyone else needs to get on board)

4. Invite a speaker who can do a great job getting everyone to truly understand the pain that bullying and cyberbullying cause, and that it has got to stop at your school[60]

5. Invite a DJ who can create a party atmosphere and once again get everyone pumped up about belonging to the school, being a Hornet or Titan or Warrior, and doing the right thing (even when it's hard)

The objective isn't to preach, or lecture, or drone on and on with a furrowed brow about how kids shouldn't bully each other. They know that. The objective is to create a formal event at your school where everyone can get together and rally around a cause and, honestly, have a fun and memorable time (with some thought provoking built in). This requires a delicate balance to the content, and a strategic approach to the structure, of the event, but it is very doable.

QUESTIONS FOR REFLECTION

Have you spearheaded an anti-bullying and/or pro-kindness pep rally at your school? Has it been successful? Did it fall short? What did you learn from the experience, and what do you think about the idea and its value in your specific school environment?

27

Student Plays to Combat Bullying

Sameer Hinduja

We are always interested in sharing cool ideas that schools are using to promote positive climates and reduce peer conflict and bullying.[61] One idea that has worked very well in some communities is the creation and performance of a school play with social-norming messages interwoven in the fabric of its story line.[62] It can include one or several different skits to deliver the actual social norms message of positive online behavior to students in a creative, relatable, and hard-hitting manner. This production can travel to classrooms within the school, be presented to the entire student body or community, or be shown as part of after-school and/or extracurricular youth programming.

A skit might include one character who is sexting a boy she has a crush on while another character, who is her friend, explains that the behavior is not "cool."[63] The mere mention that other students do not sext may be sufficient motivation to refrain from the behavior. Additionally, the play can be made interactive as the actors can solicit suggestions from the audience and then improvise on these to convey the appropriate social-norming message. The skits should be fun and interesting to watch, but they should also be direct and to the point and focus mostly on positive uses of technology among the student body. It is up to the creative talent of the drama department to determine how best to present it with props, acting, and a script. If done well, a theatrical production involving fellow students has the potential to have a positive and lasting impact on the entire student body.

One of our colleagues, Nathan Jeffrey, director of education and outreach for Taproot Theatre Company in Seattle, Washington, recently shared his passion about the value of these anti-bullying plays with us.[64] His company has been touring social-issue plays to schools in the Northwest for almost 30 years, and serves over 90,000 students each year. In the 1980s, the group focused on drug and alcohol issues, and it has covered a variety of other relevant topics that have significantly impacted the adolescent population over time. Most recently, the company has wanted to zero in on cyberbullying since a growing number of school violence incidents seemingly stem from online disagreements and dramas.

Back in 2008, Taproot Theatre premiered a show called *New Girl*, a five-character drama in which Rachel, a new student at Clements High School, is pressured into participating in hate and harassment against of one of her classmates via text and Facebook. It was tremendously successful in secondary schools, had over 210 performances between 2008 and 2011, and received great press in the media. Since then, the company has commissioned a new show to help improve school climate titled *Don't Tell Jessica*, which specifically addresses student interactions via social media.

Nathan states:

> *Our plays are designed to spark discussion at a schoolwide level and create a common frame of reference for members of the school community to talk about the problem. Our shows can empower students who are targeted by bullying to find an ally who can assist them in addressing the problem. Students who exhibit bullying behavior get the much-needed opportunity to see the face of the person getting bullied and can begin to empathize with that person's pain.*

One of the cool things about Taproot Theatre's productions is that the company provides its scripts for sale to any schools that desire to perform them themselves. I also love that Taproot provides pre- and postshow discussion questions to facilitate further dialogue and encourage youth to dive deeper into the most prominent themes of the play. This helps students brainstorm and role-play what they would actually do in certain situations as targets, aggressors, or witnesses. Moreover, a primary goal is to encourage the identification of preventive strategies and solutions that can be deployed across the campus and contribute to a healthier, safer, and more joyful environment. Fundamentally, the plays are meant to instill hope in youth, and to motivate them to work together and build a community in which everyone feels safe, and is respected and valued.

QUESTIONS FOR REFLECTION

Can you identify a handful of students and a staff member who have the skill set necessary to write and perform a skit or play that poignantly depicts an area of teen technology misuse, and teaches a positive message? How can you provide them with the symbolic and substantive support they need to take this idea and run with it?

28

Educators, Students, and Conversations About Technology Misuse

Sameer Hinduja

As the use of social media among youth has increased, school staff have become well aware that what happens online often significantly impacts the environment at school and the ability of students to learn. It is also true that what goes on at school influences the nature and content of student interactions while away from school. That means that a lack of connectedness, belongingness, peer respect, school spirit, and other climate components may very well increase the likelihood of technology misuse off campus by teens.

We are huge on the importance of creating and maintaining a positive school climate, so we wanted to study this relationship through our research. In a large-scale study involving a number of middle and high schools in one major school district, we found that where a better climate was reported by students, there were also fewer cyberbullying and sexting incidents.[65] To reiterate, schools that were rated by students to have relatively "low" school climate had more reports of cyberbullying and sexting than those rated as "medium" or "high."

EDUCATORS' EFFORTS MATTER

Relatedly, the data also revealed that teachers who talk about these issues with students are making a difference. Even though almost half (46%) of students said their teacher never talked to them about being safe on the computer and 69% of students said their teacher never talked to them about using a cell phone responsibly, when these conversations happen, they seem to have a positive impact. Students who told us that a teacher had talked to them about being safe on the computer were significantly less likely to report cyberbullying others.

> Teachers who talk about these issues with their students are making a difference.

Also, those who told us that a teacher had recently talked to them about using their cell phone responsibly were significantly less likely to say that they had sent a sext to another student. Of course, the content of those conversations is also important. Once again, we call for more research to clarify what works in terms of teachers talking with students about using their devices safely and responsibly.

STUDENTS REMAIN RELUCTANT TO REPORT

It is also noteworthy that less than 10% of targets of cyberbullying told a teacher or another adult at school about their experience (about 19% of the targets of traditional bullying told an adult at school). Much of the reluctance of students to report these kinds of behaviors stems from their skepticism that the adult will actually do anything useful to stop the behavior. In fact, most students we speak to suggest that telling a teacher (or another adult) will often make matters worse.

Interestingly, 75% of students in our study felt that the teachers at their school took bullying seriously, but fewer students (66%) felt that the teachers at their school took cyberbullying seriously. So, clearly, adults in schools have some work to do to convince students that these problems can be resolved effectively. How can a school hope to establish a positive environment if students are afraid or hesitant to talk to adults about these issues? This is just one aspect of school climate that must be corrected if administrators hope to develop and maintain a setting in which youth can freely learn and thrive.

EXPECTATION OF DISCIPLINE

In our most recent research, we asked students to tell us how likely it would be for someone at their school to be caught and punished for cyberbullying. In general, about half (51%) of the students said that it was likely that a student from their school would be punished for cyberbullying. To note, this number dropped to less than 40% among the students who had actually been victims of cyberbullying.

When we examined this question in light of student perceptions of their school environments, we found that youth who rated their school climate as "high" (or more positive) reported a higher likelihood of a response by educators. Specifically, 65% of the students at these schools also believed that those who cyberbullied others would be punished, compared to only 35% of students at schools where the climate was rated "low." Here again, the quality of the climate at school shapes student perceptions of accountability.

WHAT IS THE TAKE-HOME POINT OF THIS RESEARCH?

Overall, there are clearly fewer behavioral problems and higher academic performance in schools with a positive climate, but the influence of climate extends beyond the school walls. Students who feel they are part of a welcoming environment will largely refrain from engaging in behaviors that could risk damaging the positive relationships they have at school.

> Students who feel they are part of a welcoming environment will largely refrain from engaging in behaviors that could risk damaging the positive relationships they have at school.

According to John Shindler, director of the Western Alliance for the Study of School Climate,

You can't separate climate from instruction. You can't separate climate from leadership. You can't separate climate from the purposeful things you do to build a relationship with students. If a school is doing great on one thing, it tends to all fall in line.[66]

Now that we better understand the online experiences of our students, and know that the climate at school is related to those experiences, the next step is to work to transform our classrooms and schools into places where students feel safe, respected, involved, and connected. The resources at cyberbullying.org and in our book, *School Climate 2.0* can provide you with a road map for doing just that.[67] Even though it is not an easy path to travel, we are confident that you will not be disappointed when your efforts materialize into happier students and staff and an overall better place to learn and teach.

QUESTIONS FOR REFLECTION

How would you currently rate the climate you have at your school; poor, average, good, or great? Are students receiving appropriate messages from teachers and administrators about safe and responsible technology use? What are you intentionally doing to improve the climate and promote connectedness, belongingness, morale, and better relationships on campus?

ENDNOTES

1. White House. (2011, March 10). President and First Lady call for a united effort to address bullying. *Office of the Press Secretary*. Retrieved from https://www.whitehouse.gov/the-press-office/2011/03/10/president-and-first-lady-call-united-effort-address-bullying

2. Martinson, R. (1974). *What works? Questions and answers about prison reform.* Retrieved from http://www.nationalaffairs.com/doclib/20080527_197403502whatworksquestionsandanswersaboutprisonreformrobertmartinson.pdf

3. Ibid., p. 25.

4. For more data, see http://sentencingproject.org/doc/publications/inc_Trends_in_Corrections_Fact_sheet.pdf

5. Sneed, T. (2015, February, 12). Mass incarceration didn't lower crime, but can Congress be convinced? *U.S. News*. Retrieved from http://www.usnews.com/news/articles/2015/02/12/mass-incarceration-didnt-lower-crime-but-can-congress-be-convinced

6. Espelage, D. L. (2013). Why are bully prevention programs failing in U.S. schools? *Journal of Curriculum and Pedagogy, 10*, 121–124.

7. Jeong, S., & Lee, B. H. (2013). A multilevel examination of peer victimization and bullying preventions in schools. *Journal of Criminology, 2013*, 1–10. Retrieved from http://www.hindawi.com/journals/jcrim/2013/735397

8. Yeager, D. S., Fong, C. L., Lee, H. Y., & Espelage, D. L. (2015). Declines in efficacy of anti-bullying programs among older adolescents: Theory and a three-level meta-analysis. *Journal of Applied Developmental Psychology, 37*, 36–51.

9. Finkelhor, D., Vanderminden, J., Turner, H., Shattuck, A., & Hamby, S. (2014). Youth exposure to violence prevention programs in a national sample. *Child Abuse & Neglect, 38*, 677–686.

10. Ttofi, M. M., & Farrington, D. P. (2011). Effectiveness of school-based programs to reduce bullying: A systematic and meta-analytic review. *Journal of Experimental Criminology*, *7*, 27–56.

11. Finkelhor, D., Vanderminden, J., Turner, H., Shattuck, A., & Hamby, S. (2014). Youth exposure to violence prevention programs in a national sample. *Child Abuse & Neglect*, *38*, 683.

12. Ibid., p. 680.

13. Martinson, R. (1974). What works? Questions and answers about prison reform. *Public Interest*, 35, 22–35.

14. Wilson, J. Q. (1980). What works? Revisited: New findings on criminal rehabilitation. *Public Interest*, *61*, 3–17; Ttofi, M. M., & Farrington, D. P. (2011). Effectiveness of school-based programs to reduce bullying: A systematic and meta-analytic review. *Journal of Experimental Criminology*, *7*, 27, 45.

15. Perlus, J. G., Brooks-Russell, A., Wang, J., & Iannotti, R. J. (2014). Trends in bullying, physical fighting, and weapon carrying among 6th- through 10th-grade students from 1998 to 2010: Findings from a national study. *American Journal of Public Health*, *104*, 1100–1106.

16. U.S. Department of Justice, Office of Justice Programs, & Bureau of Justice Statistics. (2014). *National Crime Victimization Survey: School Crime Supplement, 2013*. Ann Arbor, MI: Inter-University Consortium for Political and Social Research. Retrieved from http://www.icpsr.umich.edu/icpsrweb/ICPSR/studies/34980

17. Centers for Disease Control and Prevention. (2012, June 8). Youth risk behavior surveillance—United States, 2011. *Surveillance Summaries (MMWR)*, *61*(4), 1–162. Retrieved from http://www.cdc.gov/mmwr/pdf/ss/ss6104.pdf

18. Finkelhor, D., Vanderminden, J., Turner, H., Shattuck, A., & Hamby, S. (2014). Youth exposure to violence prevention programs in a national sample. *Child Abuse & Neglect*, *38*, 677–686.

19. Cyberbullying Research Center. (2010, January 27). *Social norms and cyberbullying among students*. Retrieved from http://cyberbullying.org/social-norms-and-cyberbullying-among-students

20. Hinduja, S., & Patchin, J. (2012). *School climate 2.0: Preventing cyberbullying and sexting one classroom at a time*. Thousand Oaks, CA: Corwin.

21. Kingsland, R. L. (2014, September 23). Some say anti-bullying program goes too far. *Mail Tribune*. Retrieved from http://www.mailtribune.com/article/20140923/NEWS/140929897/101067/NEWS; National School Boards Association. (2014, July 8). Father of bullied student who committed suicide sues Illinois district and producers of anti-bullying video. *Legal Clips*.

22. Patchin, J. W., & Hinduja, S. (2014). *Words wound: Delete cyberbullying and make kindness go viral*. Minneapolis, MN: Free Spirit.

23. Cyberbullying Research Center. (2014, July 18). *Empower bystanders to improve school climate*. Retrieved from http://cyberbullying.org/empower-bystanders-to-improve-school-climate

24. See cyberbullying.org/laws and Section III of this book.

25. Pratt, T. C., Cullen, F. T., Blevins, K. R., Daigel, L. E., & Madensen, T. D. (2006). The empirical status of deterrence theory: A meta-analysis. In F. T. Cullen, J. P. Wright, & K. R. Blevins (Eds.), *Taking stock: The status*

of criminological theory, advances in criminological theory (Vol. 15, pp. 367–396). New Brunswick, NJ: Transaction.

26. Ruder, D. B. (2008, September–October). The teen brain. *Harvard.* Retrieved from http://harvardmagazine.com/2008/09/the-teen-brain.html

27. Hinduja, S., & Patchin, J. W. (2013). Social influences on cyberbullying behaviors among middle and high school students. *Journal of Youth and Adolescence, 42,* 711–722.

28. H.R. 1966 (111th): Megan Meier Cyberbullying Prevention Act. (2009–2010). Retrieved from https://www.govtrack.us/congress/bills/111/hr1966

29. Maimon, D., Antonaccio, O., & French, M. T. (2012). Severe sanctions, easy choice? Investigating the role of school sanctions in preventing adolescent violent offending. *Criminology, 50,* 495–524. doi:10.1111/j.1745-9125.2011.00268.x

30. Gregory, A., & Corneli, D. (2009). "Tolerating" adolescent needs: Moving beyond zero tolerance policies in high school. *Theory Into Practice, 48,* 106–113. Retrieved from http://www.tandfonline.com/doi/abs/10.1080/00405840902776327; American Psychological Association Zero Tolerance Task Force. (2008, December). Are zero tolerance policies effective in the schools? An evidentiary review and recommendations. *American Psychologist, 63,* 852–862. Retrieved from http://www.ncbi.nlm.nih.gov/pubmed/19086747

31. Braithwaite, J. (1989). *Crime, shame, and reintegration.* Cambridge, UK: Cambridge University Press.

32. Ibid.

33. O'Malley, P. M., & Bachman, J. G. (1983, March). Self-esteem: Change and stability between ages 13 and 23. *Developmental Psychology, 19,* 257–268. Retrieved from http://psycnet.apa.org/journals/dev/19/2/257/

34. Dolak, K. (2012, February 21). Tommy Jordan, who shot daughter's laptop, defends himself. *ABC News.* Retrieved from http://abcnews.go.com/blogs/headlines/2012/02/tommy-jordan-who-shot-daughters-laptop-defends-himself/

35. Llorens, I. (2012, April 25). Denise Abbott, Ohio mom, uses Facebook photo to punish teenage daughter (Video). *Huffpost Parents.* Retrieved from http://www.huffingtonpost.com/2012/04/25/denise-abbott-mom-facebook-photo-punishment_n_1452661.html

36. Cyberbullying Research Center. (2012, May 1). Cyberbullying your own kids to punish them. Retrieved from http://cyberbullying.org/cyberbullying-your-own-kids-to-punish-them/

37. Hinduja, S., & Patchin, J. W. (2013). Social influences on cyberbullying behaviors among middle and high school students. *Journal of Youth and Adolescence, 42,* 711–722.

38. Hirschi, T. (1969). *Causes of delinquency.* Berkeley: University of California Press.

39. Wlodkowski, R. J. (1983). *Motivational opportunities for successful teaching.* Phoenix, AZ: Universal Dimensions.

40. Cohen, J. (2006). Social, emotional, ethical, and academic education: Creating a climate for learning, participation in democracy, and well-being. *Harvard Educational Review*, 76, 201–237. Retrieved from http://hepgjournals.org/doi/abs/10.17763/haer.76.2.j44854x1524644vn

41. Hinduja, S., & Patchin, J. (2012). *School climate 2.0: Preventing cyberbullying and sexting one classroom at a time*. Thousand Oaks, CA: Corwin.

42. Klein, J., Cornell, D., & Konold, T. (2012, September). Relationships between bullying, school climate, and student risk behaviors. *School Psychology Quarterly, 27*, 154–169. Retrieved from http://psycnet.apa.org/journals/spq/27/3/154/; Thapa, A., Cohen, J., Higgins-D'Alessandro, A., & Guffey, S. (2012). School climate research summary: August 2012. *School Climate Brief*, No. 3. New York, NY: National School Climate Center. Retrieved from https://www.schoolclimate.org/climate/documents/policy/sc-brief-v3.pdf

43. Dawn, R. (2015, September 3). The unexpected advantage of giving your child a unique name. *Today*. Retrieved from http://www.today.com/parents/unexpected-advantage-giving-your-child-unique-name-t42206

44. Ybarra, M. L., & Mitchell, K. J. (2004). Online aggressor/targets, aggressors, and targets: A comparison of associated youth characteristics. *Journal of Child Psychology and Psychiatry, 45*, 1308–1316.

45. Privacy breach or public safety? Teens' Facebook posts monitored by school district. (2013, September 16). *NBC News*. Retrieved from http://www.nbcnews.com/technology/privacy-breach-or-public-safety-teens-facebook-posts-monitored-school-8C11167659

46. Madden, M., Lenhart, A., Cortesi, S., Gasser, U., Duggan, M., Smith, A., & Beaton, M. (2013, May 21). *Teens, social media, and privacy.* Pew Research Center. Retrieved from http://www.pewinternet.org/2013/05/21/teens-social-media-and-privacy

47. Patchin, J. W., & Hinduja, S. (2010). Changes in adolescent online social networking behaviors from 2006 to 2009. *Computers in Human Behavior, 26*, 1818–1821.

48. Hinduja, S., & Patchin, J. (2012). *School climate 2.0: Preventing cyberbullying and sexting one classroom at a time*. Thousand Oaks, CA: Corwin.

49. Davis, S., & Nixon, C. (2010). *Youth voice project: Student insights into bullying and peer mistreatment*. Champaign, IL: Research Press.

50. Patchin, J. W., & Hinduja, S. (2015, May 1). *Summary of our cyberbullying research (2004–2015)*. Cyberbullying Research Center. Retrieved from http://cyberbullying.org/summary-of-our-cyberbullying-research

51. Hinduja, S., & Patchin, J. W. (2007). Offline consequences of online victimization: School violence and delinquency. *Journal of School Violence, 6*(3), 89–112; Hinduja, S., & Patchin, J. W. (2009, July 30). *Cyberbullying research summary: Emotional and psychological consequences.* Cyberbullying Research Center. Retrieved from http://cyberbullying.org/cyberbullying-research-summary-emotional-and-psychological-consequences; Hinduja, S., & Patchin, J. W. (2010, July 1). *Cyberbullying research summary: Cyberbullying and self-esteem.* Cyberbullying Research Center. Retrieved from http://cyberbullying.org/cyberbullying-research-summary-cyberbullying-and-self-esteem; Hinduja, S., & Patchin, J. W. (2010, July 1). *Cyberbullying research summary: Cyberbullying and strain.* Cyberbullying Research Center. Retrieved from http://cyberbullying.org/cyberbullying-research-summary-cyberbullying-and-strain; Hinduja, S., & Patchin, J. W. (2010, July 1). *Cyberbullying research*

summary: Cyberbullying and suicide. Cyberbullying Research Center. Retrieved from http://cyberbullying.org/cyberbullying-research-summary-cyberbullying-and-suicide

52. Hinduja, S., & Patchin, J. W. (2011). Cyberbullying: A review of the legal issues facing educators. *Preventing School Failure: Alternative Education for Children and Youth, 55,* 71–78.

53. Ali, R. (2010, October 26). "Dear colleague" letter. U.S. Department of Education, Office for Civil Rights. Retrieved from http://www2.ed.gov/about/offices/list/ocr/letters/colleague-201010.pdf

54. Ibid.; Cyberbullying Research Center. (2012, December 20). *Anthony Zeno v. Pine Plains Central School District.* Retrieved from http://cyberbullying.org/anthony-zeno-v-pine-plains-central-school-district

55. Hinduja, S., & Patchin, J. W. (2012). *School climate 2.0: Preventing cyberbullying and sexting one classroom at a time.* Thousand Oaks, CA: Corwin.

56. *Barr v. Lafon*, 538 F.3d 554 (6th Cir. 2008). Retrieved from http://www.ca6.uscourts.gov/opinions.pdf/08a0305p-06.pdf

57. Hinduja, S., & Patchin, J. W. (2015). *Cyberbullying legislation and case law: Implications for school policy and practice.* Cyberbullying Research Center. Retrieved from http://cyberbullying.org/cyberbullying-fact-sheet-a-brief-review-of-relevant-legal-and-policy-issues

58. Cyberbullying Research Center. (2012, August 31). *A positive school climate makes everything possible.* Retrieved from http://cyberbullying.org/a-positive-school-climate-makes-everything-possible

59. Weng, H., Fox, D., Shackman, A., Bussan, D., & Davidson, R. J. (2014). *Changing your brain and generosity through compassion meditation training.* Retrieved from http://investigatinghealthyminds.org/cihmProjUnderstandingImpact.html#changingYourBrain

60. For more information, see Chapters 19 and 20.

61. Hinduja, S., & Patchin, J. W. (2012). *School climate 2.0: Preventing cyberbullying and sexting one classroom at a time.* Thousand Oaks, CA: Corwin.

62. Cyberbullying Research Center. (2010, January 27). *Social norms and cyberbullying among students.* Retrieved from http://cyberbullying.org/social-norms-and-cyberbullying-among-students

63. Hinduja, S., & Patchin, J. W. (2010). *Sexting: A brief guide for educators and parents.* Cyberbullying Research Center. Retrieved from http://cyberbullying.org/sexting-a-brief-guide-for-educators-and-parents/

64. Visit http://taproottheatre.org

65. Hinduja, S., & Patchin, J. W. (2012). *School climate 2.0: Preventing cyberbullying and sexting one classroom at a time.* Thousand Oaks, CA: Corwin.

66. Stover, D. (2005). Climate and culture: Why your board should pay attention to the attitudes of students and staff. *American School Board Journal, 192*(12), 30–33.

67. See also Hinduja, S., & Patchin, J. (2012). *School climate 2.0: Preventing cyberbullying and sexting one classroom at a time.* Thousand Oaks, CA: Corwin.

PART V

RATIONAL RESPONSES TO BULLYING

What Works and What Doesn't

(Continued)

29

Anonymous Reporting for Bullying and Cyberbullying Incidents

Sameer Hinduja

Justin and I strongly believe in the value of anonymous reporting systems in schools. Our experiences working with students across the United States have taught us that they want to speak up and let adults know what is going on (both offline and online), but they are very nervous that it will backfire. They don't know whom specifically to go to, they don't want it to lead to them being the next target, and they don't want to be identified and considered a "tattletale," "narc," or "rat."

Students appreciate when schools implement and provide anonymous reporting mechanisms, and these systems greatly benefit educators who need to know what is occurring outside of their immediate purview. In addition, at least 11 states require that schools allow anonymous reporting by students of bullying.[1] These states have seen the value of these systems enough to formally compel their use.

I have been working with Principal Ryan Brock over at De Portola Middle School in San Diego, California, for the last few years, and one of the reasons we've kept in touch has to do with anonymous reporting. The educators at De Portola—like many others—felt heartbroken by the all-too-frequent accounts from students that the help they needed came too late or not at all, or that they were forced to change schools instead of receiving assistance from the administrators and educators at their current school. The educators there knew that middle school is a particularly difficult time in a child's developmental trajectory, and wanted to figure out a clear and powerful way to show their students that they truly care. Everyone seems to be looking for a "best practice" to help stem the tide of peer mistreatment and victimization; as you'll see, this one truly seems to bear much fruit.

It became clear that the school needed to provide a different anonymous means for students to report an incident than the then available "Bully Report" drop boxes around campus.[2] Unfortunately, those simply were not effective in their experience, perhaps because they were not available after school hours, and students would rather text or type in their reports privately. As such, the school chose to create an online form that would be embedded on its website. To be sure, the form is not *perfectly* anonymous, in that it records the sender's IP address, but from a student's perspective, this has not been a deterrent. No student has ever asked about this aspect of the submission process, and administrators have never used such information to try to identify who sent in a report (but perhaps would work with the police to do so if they received any indication of an immediate threat to someone's safety).

The form provides a simple and effective means for students to report incidents that they are not comfortable reporting in person. Designed to be simple but include the critical questions that allow for documentation of a crime, as well as remain comfortable for a student to complete, the form is distributed via weekly school announcements, a message sent home to parents, and assemblies in front of the student body. It also has become a common occurrence for teachers to ask students to redirect their verbal account of an incident to the online tool. This allows for thoughtful reflection and documentation, and of course helps the school keep a paper trail instead of leaving much to memory.

In the year immediately after the implementation of the form, the school received around 144 submissions, including 3 false reports. While this is a tremendous number of reports for a school of 1,100 students, the school believed that the time spent in follow-up and investigation is well worth the payoff of students feeling safe at school. In fact, the number of reports has been manageable and also led to more *preventive* rather than *punitive* actions, an unexpected but valuable outcome because the school wants to build and maintain an environment oriented toward the positive, not the negative.

The reports the school receives through the anonymous online form range from online harassment in cases where students have sent threatening messages on social media, to cases of students pressuring others for money during their lunch period. Some submissions are reports of name calling or "he kicked me" during class time in situations where the student does not report the issue to the teacher. That said, the vast majority of reports from students have been legitimate instances where they needed support in dealing with a difficult situation. Interestingly, these required only a small amount of time to investigate and respond to. Forms of support might include mediation between students who have had a disagreement, increased supervision during lunch periods to deter students from demanding money from others, changing the direction of on-campus cameras to observe acts of bullying in heretofore less visible areas, or parent contact to notify families that their student has been engaging in cyberbullying or another online misbehavior.

The report on page 148 is an example of one that we recently received from a young man. It shows a clear case of bullying and an instance in which intervention could prevent a possible instance of violence. This report allowed the school to intervene and stop this cycle of behavior and prevent a retaliatory fight or worse. The administrators approached this issue by sharing the report with the student and encouraging him to reflect on the impact of his behavior. As for so many other aggressive students, this behavior stemmed from other students bullying him. To this day, the school makes it a point to give all students repeated personal reminders to be considerate of others and to always report any instances of bullying.

Many schools are looking for a solution to really help stem the tide of bullying among their students. Ryan would recommend that all educators strongly consider the approach of an online reporting mechanism, and deems it not only important but completely necessary. He reminded me that we have all been in situations where we felt caught between the consequences of calling for help and the consequences of suffering in silence. In most cases, a simple web-based tool offers a new path to *safety* that does not include the consequences from either path previously available.

1. I am a: *Student*

2. During this incident I was a: *Victim*

3. What is your name? (optional) *[No Answer Entered]*

4. What grade are you in? *7*

5. What is the name of the student you would like to report? *[Redacted]*

6. If you do not know the name of the student, please describe the person. *[No Answer Entered]*

7. Where did this incident take place? *In class*

8. Please describe the incident.

   [Redacted] has annoyed me and he always knocks down my backpack from the back of my chair anytime he walks by also he mocks me when i tell him to stop annoying me

9. Were there witnesses to this incident? *No*

10. What are the names of the witnesses? *[No Answer Entered]*

11. Please rate the severity of this incident from your perspective, 1 being minor incident but unacceptable to 5 being major incident, could result in retaliation or violence. *Severity: 3*

12. Please describe the frequency with which this type of incident occurs. *On a regular basis*

13. How do you feel about this incident or person? (Examples: they are annoying, I hate them, I want to hurt them, they don't make me mad I just want it to stop . . . etc.) *I hate him and all of his bully friends and feel as if I have to do something physically to them to stop this so if you don't solve this it might just come to that*

14. Did this or other incidents make you feel like harming yourself or others? *Yes*

15. Would you like to speak with a counselor? *No*

16. What else would you like us to know about this incident? (optional) *Stop this now him and his friends they all bully my friends and I at lunch and it needs to stop now and if you guys can't do anything it might just come to the worst. ps. If you find out who this is don't say anything to me at all or I won't be able to trust the staff and will have to solve things myself*

QUESTIONS FOR REFLECTION

What mechanisms do you currently have in place for anonymous reporting by students? Can they be improved to facilitate greater participation, more honest reports, and better student–educator communication across the school?

30

Setting Up a Free Bullying and Cyberbullying Reporting System With Google Voice

Sameer Hinduja

In Chapter 29, I shared about the utility and value of anonymous reporting systems, and I strongly advocate for them whenever I have the opportunity to speak to educators on prevention of bullying. Based on your own observations, I am sure you'd agree with me that youth are much more comfortable texting or typing—especially when it relates to giving emotionally laden statements or sharing stories of a sensitive or delicate nature with an adult (such as a teacher, counselor, or administrator). Not only do these systems cater to the preferred method of communication for kids; they also offer confidentiality to the person providing the report. Furthermore, they help to empower youth to be agents of change and stand up for themselves or for others who are being victimized. Finally, these systems allow for real-time reporting, can alert you to minor situations before they become major, and can provide a tangible "paper trail" of documentation for each and every issue made known.

> Youth are much more comfortable texting or typing—especially when it relates to giving emotionally laden statements or sharing stories of a sensitive or delicate nature with an adult.

Before I continue, I want to make a very important point. Schools sometimes hesitate to set up these systems because they are concerned about false positives. They assume that students will screw around with the system and make all sorts of ridiculous, juvenile reports and waste everyone's time. They even wonder if some students will attempt to bully others by reporting them as aggressors—all legitimate possibilities, but largely unfounded. Every school we have worked with that has implemented an anonymous reporting system has said that, yes, it might receive a few insincere reports a year, but the vast majority are legitimate and provide extremely helpful information to consider. The bottom line is that these systems allow students to be the eyes and ears of the school community to keep educators in the loop about issues they really must be aware of. And getting in front of these issues—or incendiary sparks, if you will pardon the metaphor—can definitely keep them from flaring up into a blazing inferno.

Whenever I spend time with youth at schools, I am reminded that they honestly do want to speak up. *They do.* The problem is, they just don't know how to do so safely and in a way that feels comfortable. Plus, they are concerned about the possible fallout (being found out, labeled a tattletale, or targeted with retaliation). It is up to schools, then, to create and provide safe mechanisms for reporting, and to have policies and procedures in place to reduce as much as possible the potential for that fallout.

A number of commercial services to which school districts can subscribe provide this functionality. Some are fantastic, well developed, and even equipped with more advanced features—and therefore worth checking out. However, since many school districts cannot afford to subscribe to a commercial service, or may want a solution with a smaller footprint, I wanted to share how they might provide a similar tool to their student community through Google Voice at no cost. I believe it does a great job of what we want it to do: field private reports from the student body to alert the school about situations it should investigate.

HOW IT WORKS

The system is built around a main phone number created through a new Google Voice account and then shared with the entire student body as a tip line or report line. The system then disseminates the student voice mails (rare) and texts (frequent) to school personnel such as the assistant principal, the counselor, or the school police officer for investigation and follow-up. Voice mails can be sent as a sound file or even be transcribed into text and then e-mailed to a specified address. Texts can be forwarded to a specific e-mail (or multiple e-mails) as well.

All point people (administrators, law enforcement, etc.) who want to access the tip line will have to download the Google Voice app to their phone or tablet (Android or iOS devices). Once they download the app, they must configure it with the same settings as the Google Voice tip line (e.g., the same log-in and password). Then the point person can respond to texts and calls from tipsters *from within the app*, and only the tip line number (as opposed to the point person's actual phone number) will be displayed on outgoing texts. This is critical, because it maintains the confidentiality and privacy of the administrators and law enforcement who respond to tips from their personal devices.

WHO RESPONDS TO TIPS?

Typically, each school should assign a point person to deal with the reports as they come in. Specific responses can be based on offense seriousness; most are addressable by intervention from an administrator or counselor. However, if the matter is more serious (e.g., involves threats, sexually explicit pictures of minors, coercion, blackmail, viable evidence of other criminal activity), the school police officer or local law enforcement department should be notified to intercede.

WHAT SHOULD BE REPORTED?

In discussing the reporting system with students, it should be stressed that no issue is too small. We want students to use these systems extensively and to let the school know if anything is amiss that should be investigated. Of course, schools must clearly convey that students should report actual emergencies to the police via 911 or another method. While the purpose here is to encourage the use of anonymous reporting when bullying is involved, schools should welcome the efforts of students to keep them in the loop whenever they notice, witness, or otherwise become aware of

- abuse at home (or elsewhere),
- concerns about a fellow student (self-harm, suicidal ideation, etc.),
- criminal activity (drugs, extortion, theft, vandalism, rape, etc.),
- fights, and
- general threats to campus safety or the campus environment.

IS THE SYSTEM TRULY ANONYMOUS?

In a word, no. Anyone who calls or texts the tip line will have his or her phone number recorded. Typically, though, if the tipster does not want to reveal his or her identity, it is difficult to determine who provided the tip because the school cannot readily cross-reference a database of student cell phone numbers (schools typically only maintain a database of their students' parent/guardian contact information). Googling a tipster's phone number also rarely reveals any identifying information unless the student has posted it across the web and on publicly accessible social media pages. As such, the system definitely allows for a strong measure of privacy.

OTHER POINTS TO REMEMBER

- When responding to students' tips via text, be sure to sign your name. Remember, they will not be able to see your actual phone number but instead will see the phone number of the tip line.
- The school, when responding, should always thank the tipster for the information, commend him or her for caring about the safety of the community, and remind him or her that the report will be kept confidential.
- Because of Family Educational Rights and Privacy Act (FERPA) rules, schools should not voluntarily disclose information about certain students in their text interactions with the tipster (names, personal histories, etc.).[3]
- Always keep all interactions formal and professional, as they may serve as documentation in a case file or even court proceedings in the future. A school's point person should never be casual in a text through this system, even though it is a medium with which we all are extremely comfortable.
- Follow-up dialogue may also be held via text in this process, as the school may request more information from the tipster or the tipster may desire to share more information with the school.
- Students should be reminded that the system should not be abused. They should know this anyway, but sometimes it still needs to be articulated.

In sum, we strongly believe that every school should have a system in place that allows students who experience or observe bullying (or any inappropriate behavior) to report it in as confidential a manner as possible. It seems obvious that we should be using media that youth already prefer. In addition, being able to broach the subject without being forced to reveal one's identity or do it face-to-face may prove valuable in alerting faculty and staff to harmful student experiences, and help promote an informed response to bring positive change. Just make sure that students know about the system (use posters, messaging strategies, and other creative ways to get it out there!), and try to overcome any qualms they might have about using it.

Finally, please remember that if you decide to provide such a resource to your school community, *every* complaint should be taken seriously and thoroughly investigated. Since the use of this system does provide the paper trail I talked about earlier, it's best to make sure you've done your due diligence with all reports to avoid any claims of liability or negligence. If the school responds promptly, and if it is a good experience for the student providing the tip, he or she will let other students know—and they will use the system more often. Even better, all students will be reminded that the school truly cares about them and is implementing progressive measures to make that clear.

NOTE: On our website, we have posted a step-by-step guide in PDF format to walk educators through the process of setting up a bullying and cyberbullying reporting system with Google Voice.[4] It has clear directions and screenshots to help you, and we advise you to consider it if you don't have another system in place, and/or don't have the need or funds for a subscription-based service.

QUESTIONS FOR REFLECTION

Do you have an anonymous reporting system in place? If not, what keeps you from implementing one? Let us know if you need any help, and share with us your experiences.

31

VIDEO EVIDENCE OF BULLYING

Implications for
an Effective Response

Justin W. Patchin

In 2014, a video surfaced showing a bullying incident in Rancho Cucamonga, California.[5] The video shows 14-year-old high school freshman Kobe Nelson being pushed around by a classmate while a throng of onlookers heckle and encourage the two to fight. Several of the students can be seen recording the situation on their cell phones. It appears from the video that Kobe is simply trying to walk away, but the aggressor keeps pulling him back into the fray. Eventually Kobe is able to escape, but is later contacted by a police officer assigned to the school who inquires about the fight. He was taken to the office where he was informed that he was being suspended for two days for fighting. Presumably the other student involved was also suspended, but his sanction has not been discussed publicly.[6]

There is sadly nothing all that special or unique about this kind of incident—fights happen in schools every day, and near misses like this are without a doubt even more frequent. According to the 2014 *Indicators of*

School Crime and Safety, 8% of high school students were involved in a fight at school in 2013 (down from 12% in 2011).[7] Overall, these numbers have been dropping since the mid-1990s, but still remain at levels of concern. No data are available that quantify the number of times students walk away, as Kobe did on the day of the video.

Kobe protested his suspension, arguing that he didn't do anything wrong. When his father, Tommy Purvis, learned about the video and watched it, he saw clearly that Kobe's description of the incident was accurate—he *didn't* do anything wrong. Mr. Purvis approached school officials with the video, but they reportedly refused to watch it, saying that they already knew what had happened. The police officer assigned to the high school also apparently mocked Kobe, telling him that he should "bulk up" so he wouldn't make for such an easy target. Perhaps this was an ill-conceived attempt by the officer to lighten things up. But flippant responses like this help explain why less than 30% of the students in our surveys tell an adult about their experience with bullying.[8] Dissatisfied with the school and law enforcement response, Mr. Purvis and his son went public with the incident by posting the story, and video, online.

THE POWER OF VIDEO EVIDENCE

Video has always served as valuable evidence to enable investigators to see exactly the extent of one's involvement in a criminal incident. Remember back in 2008 when several girls lured 16-year-old Victoria Lindsay into one of their homes for the purpose of beating her up? The motive for the assault seemed to have been linked to some trash-talking by Victoria on Myspace. The assault was premeditated for the purpose of teaching her a lesson and was deliberately perpetrated in front of several cell phone cameras so that the incident could be posted on Myspace and YouTube. Several girls were charged criminally, and the chief offender, Brittini Hardcastle, who was 17 at the time of the incident, served 15 days in jail.[9] The assault was immortalized online and in a 2011 Lifetime movie (*Girl Fight*). No shortage of similar squabbles has gone viral; indeed, publicity and notoriety seems to abound when cruelty is captured in its raw and unedited form. Indeed, one wonders if Rodney King would be a household name today if not for the video that emerged of his beating by officers of the Los Angeles Police Department.[10]

With this in mind, should we encourage bystanders to record incidents of bullying when they witness it so that adults tasked with investigating can see exactly what happened? We already suggest that students to keep all evidence of cyberbullying, so reminding and allowing them to document face-to-face incidents like this can help adults sort through the details of what happened so that offending parties can be held accountable. Of course, this can be abused. There is a big difference between the teen who gleefully records an incident for the purpose of later public posting and ridicule, and the teen who quietly gathers evidence to support a friend and take to the authorities. The latter may be appropriate while the former most certainly is not (and may warrant punishment in its own right).

It is important to remember, too, that video recordings often capture only a snippet of a larger incident. In Kobe's video, we see less than 90 seconds of the interaction and have no idea what Kobe said or did to possibly instigate the altercation. Every story has multiple sides, and I wouldn't be surprised if more details emerged in that case. That said, one can examine only the available evidence, and video should always be used in combination with eyewitness interviews to put the pieces of the puzzle together correctly.

I worry, however, that were it not for the video evidence, Kobe would have had a harder time substantiating the facts of the incident. Sure, maybe a few of his friends would have stepped up and offered support for his version of the events, but no doubt other observers would have contradicted those reports, and the school would have been forced to default to offsetting penalties (punishment for both). And what kind of message would that send?

> Video should always be used in combination with eyewitness interviews to put the pieces of the puzzle together correctly.

WITH CYBERBULLYING, THERE IS ALWAYS EVIDENCE

One of the defining characteristics of cyberbullying is that there is *always* evidence. Whether it is a text, Facebook post, Instagram picture, tweet, or video, it is important to continually remind those who are being targeted, as well as those who observe it happening to others, to preserve that evidence. With face-to-face bullying, it is often one person's word against another's. Digital evidence helps to clarify who said what, and when.

I once talked with a school resource officer in Wisconsin about an incident where a student came up to him after school and said she was receiving mean text messages. The officer asked the student to bring in a copy of the messages for him to review. The next day, this student brought him a printed-out copy of the messages, which included over two pages of content. The problem was that just about every other message had been blocked out with a black Sharpie. When the officer questioned the student about the redacted messages, the student responded, "Well, those are my texts to her, and those aren't important." Of course they are important!

Adults who investigate bullying incidents need to see *all* of the information surrounding the incident so they can respond appropriately given all of the available facts.

School and law enforcement officials need to thoroughly investigate all reports of bullying so that those responsible can be properly disciplined. This is actually a lot harder to do than it sounds. First of all, many law enforcement officers lack good training on how to handle bullying (especially cyberbullying).[11] And even though school administrators are generally much better at handling these kinds of incidents, they are stretched so thin with declining budgets and increasing mandated responsibilities that they often do not have enough time to adequately investigate these reports. So they triage them as best they can, but sometimes mistakes are made. Ultimately, it is up to everyone who witnesses bullying incidents to step up and report what they see so that the correct and appropriate action can be taken.

QUESTIONS FOR REFLECTION

Do you think students should be encouraged to record incidents of bullying on their mobile devices? Why or why not? Does your school have a policy regarding students recording activities at school?

32

Law Enforcement Involvement in Bullying Incidents

Different Rules and Roles

Justin W. Patchin

In Chapter 31, I wrote about a student who was suspended for his involvement in a fight of which video evidence showed that he did not participate in a way that warranted the punishment. In fact, from all available evidence, he did exactly the right thing: walk away. Another aspect of the case that generated public scorn was the reported unprofessional treatment that the student received from the police officer assigned to the school. As mentioned, the officer evidently told the student that he should "bulk up" as a way to avoid being pushed around in the future. This got me to thinking a bit about the role of law enforcement officers in schools.

Recent data are hard to come by, but thousands of officers work in schools every day across the United States. They are mostly responsible for the safety and security of the students, staff, and visitors, but often are utilized in a variety of other roles—some of which they are inadequately prepared for. For example, school-based law enforcement officers are occasionally called on to provide instruction in the classroom (especially using pre-packaged drug, gang, or violence prevention curricula), yet they rarely receive formal training on how to teach effectively. They basically do the best they can. Moreover, officers are regularly brought in to investigate or even mediate peer conflict, yet many are not well trained in dealing with bullying incidents or even in working with kids generally. Over 80% of the school-based officers we surveyed back in 2010 said that they needed more training on how to deal with cyberbullying.[12] So what can cops contribute to the well-being of students and staff at school?

LAW ENFORCEMENT PRESENCE IN SCHOOLS: SRO VS. AD HOC MODEL

Schools with a dedicated school resource officer (SRO) assigned to their building are at an advantage when it comes to dealing with student issues that may implicate law enforcement. These officers generally have more training and experience in dealing with students and schools and their unique issues than their counterparts assigned to traditional patrol functions. Since SROs are in the schools on a continual basis, they are usually more attuned to student interpersonal relationships and the concerns of educators. The best officers know the students personally, and interact with them in a relatable way. As a result, students come to respect the police and better understand that they do more than, say, show up at their house during a domestic disturbance or issue them a citation for driving five miles per hour over the speed limit.

Unfortunately, this model is disappearing in many schools across the country as both school and municipal budgets have contracted. Historically, SROs were often funded through a combination of money from schools and cities or counties, but when one partner pulls the financial plug, the other rarely has the resources to make up the difference, and the position is usually lost. As a result, police are often called to the school only in situations where a significant (and possibly criminal) incident has occurred. Sometimes the same officer responds throughout the school year, but often the call will be directed to whomever is on duty and in the area at the time. Having a consistent contact is important from a procedural standpoint (making sure the officer is aware of the issues related to schools and students), but it also helps to have a familiar face—from the perspective of both the staff and the students.

DIFFERENT ROLES AND RESPONSIBILITIES

When it comes to responding to bullying (or any incident, really), school administrators and law enforcement officers play different yet complementary roles. Usually, law enforcement is pulled into the discussion only when an incident appears to rise to the level of a violation of criminal law. Assaults or serious substantiated threats of violence are the most common examples of the need to bring in the police. Law enforcement can also assist in investigating incidents. These officers often have more training in interviewing and evidence collection, and can evaluate evidence to determine if a crime has been committed. That said, schools should be careful when including law enforcement officers in an interview because it changes the dynamic considerably. Having a uniformed police officer stand over the shoulder of the principal while he or she asks a student about school behaviors is intimidating under any circumstance, but especially so if the officer is not regularly seen at the school.

Technically speaking, when an administrator investigates an incident, he or she does so as a representative of the school, for possible *school discipline*. If the police are involved (whether an SRO or other officer), the investigation may become one with a focus on uncovering evidence of a crime for possible *criminal punishment*. When that happens, the procedural rules change. For instance, when a school official interviews a student or searches his or her property, he or she typically only needs a reasonable belief that the student has engaged in, or possesses evidence of, a behavior that violates school policy. Very few constitutional protections are afforded to students in these cases because the school is acting *in loco parentis* (in place of parents), not as a government official for the purpose of formal punishment. When the police are involved in investigating a crime, citizens (including minors) do have certain rights.

In *Miranda v. Arizona* the U.S. Supreme Court ruled that, prior to "custodial interrogations," law enforcement officers must inform individuals suspected of committing a crime that they have specific protections.[13] We've all heard this statement before on crime shows: "You have the right to remain silent. Anything you say can be used against you in a court of law. . . . You have the right to an attorney. . . . If you can't afford one, one will be provided . . ." and so on. This standard also generally applies when officers are interviewing minors in the community, but the Kentucky Supreme Court recently raised the question of whether students should be informed of their rights when being questioned by an officer at school, or by a school administrator in the presence of an officer.[14]

The Kentucky Supreme Court reaffirmed the ability of school officials to interview students for the purpose of a possible school sanction without being required to inform them of their rights, but ruled that in circumstances where a police officer is involved and criminal charges are possible, *Miranda* warnings are required. This deviates from some previous interpretations, which basically held that if a law enforcement officer was assisting in a school investigation, the officer was beholden to the rules that applied to school officials. No doubt this issue is headed to the U.S. Supreme Court for clarification.

I have also previously written quite a bit on the different issues associated with whether an educator or a law enforcement officer can search the contents of a student cell phone (see Chapter 36). *New Jersey v. T.L.O.* states that students are protected by the Fourth Amendment to the U.S. Constitution, which protects citizens from unreasonable searches and seizures by government officials.[15] In *T.L.O.*, the Supreme Court also made it clear that the standard that law enforcement officers must reach to conduct a search (probable cause that *a crime has been committed*) is not required of educators. The standard applied to school officials is whether the search is "justified at its inception and reasonable in scope." Of course, there is a bit of subjectivity to this standard, and what appears to be reasonable for one person may not be for another. In *T.L.O.*, the Court ruled that for a search of student property to be justified, there must exist "reasonable grounds for believing that the search will turn up evidence that the student has violated or is violating either the law or the rules of the school."

These are just some of the issues, and as you can probably tell, many of the important questions have not been fully settled. Overall, officers and educators need to use their judgment about situations that might benefit from, or necessitate, law enforcement involvement. As long as there is no immediate threat of harm, it is usually best for school administrators to interview students involved in misbehavior without a law enforcement officer present. Under these circumstances, they have a lot more freedom and leeway to gather the necessary information. As soon as the administrator reaches the conclusion that a crime may have been committed, he or she should turn the investigation over to the police. We recommend that administrators have open lines of communication with local law enforcement officers (and especially SROs) so that both can respond quickly and effectively when confronted with a problem.

> As long as there is no immediate threat of harm, it is usually best for school administrators to interview students involved in misbehavior without a law enforcement officer present.

COORDINATED COMMUNITY RESPONSE

A well-trained and experienced SRO would be an asset in any school, and most administrators would (or at least should) welcome them with open arms. I have seen many amazing SROs work their magic in schools— improving safety and crisis response efforts, yes, but also enhancing police–community relations and improving the overall culture of the school and broader community.[16] The evidence concerning the effectiveness of SROs varies considerably, which isn't surprising given the diversity of personalities employed in these positions, and the varying ways in which schools utilize SROs.[17] As is frequently the case, the conclusion I reach is that more solid research is necessary.

As a criminologist who routinely teaches future cops, I know that the vast majority of law enforcement officers approach every assignment with integrity and professionalism. Some are cut out to work in schools, while others simply are not. The latter need to be pulled out because they do more harm than good. From the available evidence, the officer in the previous chapter who told the student who was being bullied to "bulk up" isn't a good fit for a school and should be reassigned. If administrators and SROs work together for the common purpose of helping youth (along with parents, of course), then great things can happen. This can fail in a lot of ways, but usually it doesn't. The high-profile anomalies will end up on the nightly news, on YouTube, or in a courtroom. But we shouldn't base our opinions on these worst cases and instead should focus on what we can do to improve the response efforts of all involved.

QUESTIONS FOR REFLECTION

What kind of relationship does your school have with local law enforcement? Do you feel the officers and school administrators clearly understand their different roles when investigating incidents of bullying? If you do not have a full-time SRO, at what point does your school bring law enforcement into an incident?

33

HOLDING PARENTS RESPONSIBLE FOR THEIR CHILD'S BULLYING

Justin W. Patchin

Without a doubt, parents have a duty to ensure that their kids do not bully others. They need to regularly remind their kids about the importance of treating others the way they would want to be treated. They should talk about how some things we might do or say to someone that seem funny at the time are actually pretty hurtful. When it comes to preventing cyberbullying, parents need to regularly check in on the online behaviors of their kids. They need to address problematic behaviors with reasonable and appropriate discipline. In general, parents need to instill in their children a moral compass that includes respecting others and always acting and interacting with integrity, whether online or offline. And they can do that in a caring and authoritative manner that encourages emotional connectedness yet demands respect and accountability. Indeed, research has shown a positive parent–child relationship makes it less likely that youth will engage in bullying behaviors, as they do not want to risk damaging the valued bond.[18]

But if parents fail to take these steps and their child bullies others, should the parents themselves be held criminally responsible?

ATTEMPT AT ACCOUNTABILITY

An ordinance approved in 2013 by the Monona, Wisconsin, Common Council allows parents of children who bully to be fined $114.[19] The city is the first in the country that we are aware of to pass such a measure. The council also amended its ordinances to incorporate existing state criminal statutes that prohibit disorderly conduct, unlawful use of a telephone or computerized communication system, and harassment. All of this sends a clear message to citizens that harassment in all of its forms is not welcome within the city limits.

In Chapter 13, I discussed the growing movement among municipalities to criminalize cyberbullying locally by enacting ordinances. As occurred in Monona, many times city ordinances simply mirror existing state laws. As I wrote in that chapter, there are a few reasons for why this move might make sense. It allows a city attorney to pursue charges against an individual even when the county-level district attorney is unwilling. It also allows for the cases to be handled in a municipal court (which Monona does have—many cities do not) rather than the state circuit court system. This has the added effect (for better or worse) of shielding violators from the public shame of being eternally listed on Wisconsin's Consolidated Court Automation Programs website for all to see.

HISTORY AND THEORY
BEHIND PARENTAL LIABILITY LAWS

Parental liability laws hold parents accountable, and financially liable, for the behavior of their children when it is deemed that the parents were negligent in their obligation to provide proper parental care and supervision. In theory, these laws make a lot of sense: the idea is to compel parents to make sure their kids aren't behaving in a reckless or delinquent manner. School law states that educators can be held liable for damages when they are found to have been *deliberately indifferent* to harassment that happens at schools.[20] Maybe it is appropriate to hold parents to the same standard. Parents who are not adequately "parenting" ought to be punished right along with their kids, right? Well, in practice, it is much more complicated.

States have long had various laws on the books that can be used to hold adults responsible for the actions of youth.[21] In 1903, Colorado was the first state to make it a crime to "contribute to the delinquency of a minor."[22] California law generally requires parents to "exercise reasonable care, supervision, protection, and control over their children."[23] Parents who fail in this mandate can be found guilty of a misdemeanor and sentenced to jail. Massachusetts law states that "a parent is under a duty to exercise reasonable care to prevent his minor child from inflicting injury, intentionally or negligently, on others."[24] In fact, some have suggested that parental responsibility laws can be traced back to 1646 when Massachusetts enacted its Stubborn Child Law, which noted that parents can be fined if their child is caught stealing.[25] Of course, the same law proclaimed that "stubborn and rebellious" sons who do not obey their parents "shall be put to death."[26]

OTHER POSSIBLE CAUSES OF, AND SOLUTIONS TO, THE PROBLEM

A number of years ago, I was involved in evaluating a truancy reduction initiative in three elementary schools in Michigan.[27] One element of the program was to hold parents accountable if their elementary-aged children did not attend school. For students younger than 12 years old whose parents *did not cooperate with school officials*, a warrant was sought for parental prosecution under the state's compulsory attendance law. The key phrase here was that the parents targeted were uncooperative (and indignant). Only 3 parents out of the nearly 300 families involved in the program fell into this category. Most were just looking for help to address a relatively simple problem that contributed to the absenteeism, like providing an alarm clock or transportation to school.

I think the same can be said when it comes to bullying. Most often, when parents learn about the bullying behaviors of their children, they will take the necessary steps to ensure that such behaviors do not continue. In some cases, they just don't know what to do, but with a little guidance, they will be fine. In very rare cases, parents simply do not recognize the bullying behavior of their children as hurtful, or worse, they may even encourage it. Parents may also completely ignore what their kids do online, even after being made aware of possible problems. Presumably, these are the types of parents toward whom parental responsibility laws are directed.

One problem I see with this approach is that it is also likely to have a result that is opposite of what was intended. We know that the quality of the parent–child relationship is integral in preventing a whole host of inappropriate behaviors. The concern is that threatening to punish a parent for the behavior of the child may serve to further weaken this relationship. Parent and child are pitted against one another when the child misbehaves: "Because of what *you* did, *I* have to pay $114!" Furthermore, anyone who has a child of his or her own or who has worked with youth in a professional capacity (I fall in both camps) knows that even the best-intentioned guardian can run into an obstinate child who refuses to follow any instructions. It would be inappropriate to hold parents responsible in situations where clearly they are doing everything they can to try to remedy the behavior. These laws are really intended to handle the opposite—when parents are doing very little to respond. Again, I feel like this happens very rarely.

RESEARCH LACKING

Unfortunately, no evaluation research has been done to assess the effectiveness of parental liability statutes, so we really do not know what kind of effect they will have. Eve Brank, a professor of law and psychology at the University of Nebraska in Lincoln, has studied parental responsibility laws in depth and told me "it's impossible to speak about whether they are a good tool or not. We know that parents certainly play an important role in raising their children, but we do not know the effect of imposing legal sanctions on them when their children are involved in illegal behavior."[28] Indeed, in the project I referred to earlier that targeted elementary absenteeism in Michigan, we were unable to follow the students long enough to determine if the threat of parental prosecution actually resulted in better attendance.[29] So we frankly just don't know if holding parents criminally or financially responsible for the behavior of their kids will result in reduced bullying.

Critics have argued hat this is simply another way to limit free speech and that the parents of outspoken youth will be punished for the protected speech of their kids.[30] If a child speaks up about his or her moral objections to homosexuality, for example, it may be construed as bullying and therefore invoke punishment for the child and now the parent as well. Even though the Monona ordinance clearly states that it does not apply to any "constitutionally protected activity or speech," there is admittedly ambiguity when it comes to defining an incident as bullying, especially when it involves contentious subjects. As adults (parents and others), it is our responsibility to teach teens to disagree, and even debate, in a civil manner.

QUESTIONS FOR REFLECTION

Should parents be held responsible for the behaviors of their kids? What consequences do you think would be most effective at encouraging them to take better care of responding to problems? Should the police and courts get involved?

34

A POTENTIAL RESPONSE TO CYBERBULLYING

Talking to the Parents of the Child Who Bullies

Justin W. Patchin

I received an e-mail from an educator who attended a recent presentation. She asked if it is advisable for the parents of cyberbullying targets to contact the parents of those doing the cyberbullying to try to resolve the situation. This can be a very tricky proposition. In theory, it seems like a very good approach, and for many parents, it can be an effective strategy. However, those who experience any form of bullying are usually terrified by the prospects of this idea. They believe that confronting the parents of the child who is responsible will only make matters worse. And it certainly can, if the conversation is not approached delicately.

The problem is that some parents confronted with accusations that their child is an aggressor may become defensive and therefore may not be receptive to your thoughts, your ideas, or any formal or informal intervention.

They might immediately put up a "wall" and become incredibly defensive. The key here really is to protect the safety of your bullied child. As a parent about to have this conversation, carefully weigh the various factors at hand and take into consideration the "totality of circumstances" (as the courts like to say). Do you know the parents? How receptive do you think they will be? Is the child who bullied your child a former friend? Have there been problems in the past? Will you as a parent have to deal with collateral damage in other social situations, if you and the parents of the aggressor interact in other environments?

Sameer has heard of an instance where the father of an aggressor "got back" at the father of a victim by embarrassing him and picking on him in front of their other friends during their weekly softball games. Of course, middle-aged male softball players sometimes demonstrate exaggerated masculinity and work to display bravado in a collective setting. The pointed "elbow-ribbing" and tongue-in-cheek comments made the father of the victim feel ostracized and emasculated, since all of the other men believed his son should have been able to handle himself like a "real man" instead of tattling to "Daddy."

Also, if the students attend the same school, it is probably a good idea to inform administrators of the situation so that they can monitor the interactions at school to make sure there is no retaliation. Moreover, I have found that school counselors are among the best at handling relationship problems and can offer advice about how to deal with what is going on. They are often willing to intervene quietly in a way that stops the harassment without unduly instigating the aggressor or his or her family.

Because each situation is different and clearly complicated, it is difficult for me to say with any certainty that confronting the parents of the child who bullied yours is a good idea. All I can say is that if you choose this approach, be sure to tread lightly and keep in mind what life was like when you were a teenager. Also consider how you would feel if someone confronted you about the behavior of your child. It is easy to say that you would listen calmly and respond appropriately, but would you? That crazy "do unto others" rule might apply to our behaviors as adults just as much as it does to our children's behavior.

QUESTIONS FOR REFLECTION

Should parents confront other parents when working through a bullying incident? If you were a parent of a child who was being bullied, would you contact the parents of the child doing the bullying? What if your child was doing the bullying?

35

Can a School Respond to Off-Campus Cyberbullying?

Justin W. Patchin

I've written about legal issues associated with schools responding to cyberbullying incidents quite often (see cyberbullying.org for more comprehensive information). Of course, the law, and our understanding of it, is constantly evolving. So I thought I would include a (relatively) simplified update with the lineage of case law that demonstrates that schools do in fact have the authority to apply reasonable discipline to students who participate in cyberbullying while away from school. Below I provide a brief summary of the rulings, but I encourage everyone to read the actual facts of each case so that you can better understand the unique context of each incident.

Tinker v. Des Moines Independent Community School District (1969): Students have free-speech rights. "A prohibition against expression of opinion, without any evidence that the rule is necessary to avoid substantial interference with school discipline or the rights of others, is not permissible under the First and Fourteenth Amendments." Students have constitutional rights under the First Amendment. Those rights, however, do not grant students the right to substantially interfere with school discipline or "the rights of other students to be secure and to be let alone."[31]

> Schools do in fact have the authority to apply reasonable discipline to students who participate in cyberbullying while away from school.

Bethel School District No. 403 v. Fraser (1986): Students' free-speech rights are limited while at school. "[T]he constitutional rights of students in public school are not automatically coextensive with the rights of adults in other settings." The Supreme Court ruled that there is a substantive difference between a nondisruptive expression (such as in *Tinker*) and "speech or action that intrudes upon the work of the schools or the rights of other students."[32]

Davis v. Monroe County Board of Education (1999): If a school knows about harassment or other hurtful actions against students and doesn't respond effectively to prevent it from continuing, it may be held responsible. "[T]he common law, too, has put schools on notice that they may be held responsible under state law for their failure to protect students from the tortious acts of third parties."[33]

J.S. v. Bethlehem Area School District (2000): Schools can discipline students for their off-campus electronic speech (e.g., a student created a threatening web page about his algebra teacher). "[S]chool officials are justified in taking very seriously threats against faculty and other students."[34]

Wisniewski v. Board of Education of the Weedsport Central School District (2007): "[I]t was reasonably foreseeable that Wisniewski's communication would cause a disruption within the school environment. . . . The fact that Aaron's creation and transmission of the IM [AOL Instant Messaging] icon occurred away from school property does not necessarily insulate him from school discipline. We have recognized that off-campus conduct can create a foreseeable risk of substantial disruption within a school."[35]

Barr v. Lafon (2008): Schools do not need to wait for a substantial disruption to occur on campus before taking action. The U.S. Court of Appeals (6th Circuit) ruled that "appellate court decisions considering school bans on expression have focused on whether the banned conduct would likely trigger disturbances such as those experienced in the past" and pointed to the fact that the high school had even positioned law enforcement officials on campus in previous years to maintain order in an environment of racial hostility and violence.[36] Citing *Lowery v. Euverard*, the court stated that "under the *Tinker* standard a school does not need to wait until a disruption has actually occurred before regulating student speech."[37]

Kowalski v. Berkeley County Schools (2011): Schools can discipline students for their online speech, consistent with *Tinker*. "Kowalski used the Internet to orchestrate a targeted attack on a classmate, and did so in a manner that was sufficiently connected to the school environment as to implicate the

School District's recognized authority to discipline speech which 'materially and substantially interfere[s] with the requirements of appropriate discipline in the operation of the school and collid[es] with the rights of others.'"[38]

In several cases, students succeeded in their lawsuits against schools when the student was disciplined for off-campus behavior.[39] In all of these cases, however, the school was incapable of demonstrating that the off-campus behavior or speech resulted in, or had a likelihood of resulting in, a substantial disruption at school. In fact, when the 3rd Circuit Court of Appeals ruled against the schools in *Layshock* and *Blue Mountain*, Judge Kent Jordan stated, "The issue is whether the Supreme Court's decision in *Tinker* can be applicable to off-campus speech. I believe it can, and no ruling coming out today is to the contrary."[40]

Finally, it is important to point out that I regularly discuss these issues with many of the best and brightest legal minds in the United States, and many of them disagree! We are living in a challenging and uncertain time (to say the least) when it comes to education in this country, and the legal ambiguity concerning a school's authority to respond to off-campus behaviors is just one more example. The reality, in my view, is that there is no uncertainty about this issue. Schools simply do have the authority to reasonably discipline students for any behavior (whether at school or away from school) if such behavior results in, or has a high likelihood of resulting in, a substantial or material disruption at school or if the behavior infringes on the rights of other students. So the short answer to the question posed in the title of this chapter is *yes*!

QUESTIONS FOR REFLECTION

Are you aware of any cases where a school was found to be liable for damages for disciplining a student for his or her off-campus behavior that resulted in a substantial disruption at school? How do you respond to incidents of bullying that originate or occur completely away from school?

36

WHEN CAN EDUCATORS SEARCH STUDENT CELL PHONES?

Justin W. Patchin

Do students have an expectation of privacy on their cell phones while at school? The short answer to this is a qualified yes. Whether educators have the authority to search the contents of student cell phones depends on a lot of factors. The key issue in this analysis is the standard of *reasonableness*. As mentioned in Chapter 32, students are protected by the Fourth Amendment to the U.S. Constitution, which protects citizens against unreasonable searches and seizures.[41] In *T.L.O.*, the Supreme Court went on to say that the standard that law enforcement officers must reach to conduct a search (probable cause that a crime has been committed) is not required of educators. In general, the standard applied to school officials is whether the search is "justified at its inception and reasonable in scope." Of course, there is a bit of subjectivity to this guideline, and what appears to be reasonable for one person may not be for another. In *T.L.O.*, the Court ruled that for a search of student property to be justified, there must exist "reasonable grounds for believing that the search will turn up evidence that the student has violated or is violating either the law or the rules of the school." This seems to be the standard by which schools should determine whether a search of a student cell phone is allowable.

CASE LAW ON EDUCATOR SEARCHES OF CELL PHONES

A couple of cases have been decided that shed some light on how this particular standard would apply to the search of student cell phones. In the case most often cited, a teacher confiscated a student's cell phone because it was visible during class—a violation of school policy (it accidentally fell out of the student's pocket).[42] The teacher and assistant principal then searched through the cell phone's number directory and attempted to call nine other Nazareth students to determine if they too were in violation of the policy. They also accessed text and voice mail messages and communicated with the student's brother without indicating to him that they were school staff.

The court agreed that the school was justified in seizing the phone, but should not have used the phone to "catch other students' violations." In summary, the U.S. District Court in *Klump* concluded, "Although the meaning of 'unreasonable searches and seizures' is different in the school context than elsewhere, it is nonetheless evident that there must be some basis for initiating a search. A reasonable person could not believe otherwise."

In November 2010, a Mississippi federal court identified no Fourth Amendment violation when a teacher seized, and administrators reviewed, photos and text messages in a cell phone confiscated from a boy (J.W.) who used it in violation of a schoolwide ban.[43] Of course, the seizure was allowed because the school had a policy prohibiting the possession or use of cell phones at school. The issue in this case was the legitimacy of the search of the phone's contents, which included incriminating pictures of the student wearing what appeared to be gang clothing.

The court ruled that the school was justified in searching the cell phone:

> *Upon witnessing a student improperly using a cell phone at school, it strikes this court as being reasonable for a school official to seek to determine to what end the student was improperly using that phone. For example, it may well be the case that the student was engaged in some form of cheating, such as by viewing information improperly stored in the cell phone. It is also true that a student using his cell phone at school may reasonably be suspected of communicating with another student who would also be subject to disciplinary action for improper cell phone usage.*[44]

I personally believe that the Mississippi court got this case wrong. Searching the student's phone will not yield any additional evidence that he is in violation of the school's policy prohibiting possession of the phone at school. Seeing the phone in school already sufficiently established that point. The court argued that "a student's decision to violate school rules by bringing contraband on campus and using that contraband within view of teachers appropriately results in a diminished privacy expectation in that contraband." Clearly the court in *Klump* did not agree with this reasoning as the court sided with the student. And while *New Jersey v. T.L.O.* established a different search and seizure standard for educators, the Supreme Court did not in that case suggest that any policy violation whatsoever negated any expectation of privacy a student previously held. The court in *J.W.* seemed to suggest that if a student chooses to deliberately violate a school policy, that student should also be willing to shed any other constitutional protections with respect to the contraband. It should be noted, though, that the Mississippi court did attempt to distinguish the facts of *J.W.* from those of *Klump* by saying J.W. intentionally violated school policy whereas Klump accidentally violated the policy. I'm unconvinced that this should be a salient factor. Does it really matter that much if a policy is accidentally or intentionally violated? Given the many apparent contradictions between *Klump* and *J.W.* (and other student cell phone search cases), I would love to see the U.S. Supreme Court review this issue to provide much needed clarity to educators and school law enforcement officers.

WHAT IS REASONABLE?

At both ends of the continuum of circumstances, the law is fairly clear. For example, if a reputable student advises a staff member that another student has the answers to the math exam on his mobile device, this would almost certainly allow for a seizure and search by an administrator. At the other extreme, conducting a search of a cell phone that was confiscated because it was ringing in a student's backpack would likely not be allowed. Of course, there is quite a bit of gray ground in between to cover.

With all of this said, schools would be wise to include a specific statement in their policies that regulate student-owned devices brought to school. The policy should advise everyone that students who bring their own devices to school are subject to a reasonable search if suspicion arises that the device contains evidence of a violation of school policy or the law. Students, staff, parents, and law enforcement officers working in the schools need to be aware of this policy so that no one is surprised if or when certain actions are taken. Increasing numbers of schools are opening their doors and classrooms to cell phones and other mobile devices. As such, it is imperative that clarity is established in this area of case law and policy.

QUESTIONS FOR REFLECTION

Do you think educators should be allowed to search student cell phones simply when the students possess them (with possession being the sole school policy violation)? Or, should educators be allowed to search student cell phones only if they can articulate that they reasonably believe that evidence on the phone will reveal another policy violation? Do you believe the laws need to be changed in this area?

37

WHY CONFISCATING STUDENT CELL PHONES MIGHT BE A BAD IDEA

Sameer Hinduja

In previous chapters, we've talked about students bringing their personal electronic devices to school and the complications that may result.[45] On our website, we have a cell phone search checklist that may help administrators in these situations.[46] In keeping with these discussions, I wanted to take some time to focus in on *seizure*—or confiscation—of these devices while bracketing the thorny subject of search for a while. Specifically, I want to be clear and state that, even with a suspected or actual policy violation by a student, it may not be in your school's best interests to seize that student's device.

I chatted this out with Mark Trachtenbroit, principal at Kennesaw Mountain High School in Georgia.[47] He remarked that his school used to take students' personal devices when they were displayed or used between the morning bell and the afternoon bell because that contravened the formal rules the school had in place. However, it became a huge chore, leading to numerous complications involving confronting students, the huge hassle of trying to warehouse, label, and manage all of the confiscated devices, and unpleasant conversations with angry parents who demanded their kid's device be returned.

As such, the school decided that the educators would no longer confiscate phones, but just apply moderate penalties to students who broke the rules. For instance, the first violation would be a stern verbal warning. The second violation would lead to Saturday school. The third violation would lead to in-school suspension. This tended to work in that it reduced the number of negative outcomes but seemed to be a less-than-ideal solution. Administrators felt they were, as they say, cutting off their nose to spite their face because punishing teens in this way kept them out of the classroom where they would be learning. This directly ties into the No Child Left Behind Act and the adequate yearly progress measurement that allows the U.S. Department of Education to determine how each school and school district is doing when it comes to properly educating U.S. students (to do well academically on standardized tests) and meeting annual targets for reading, math, and graduation.[48] The consequences for failing to meet these goals and targets are simply not worth risking, and it just doesn't make sense to sternly discipline kids in the 21st century for being 21st century kids. That is, the big-picture costs of punishing teens for being tethered to their technology are not worth potentially compromising the achievement of federally mandated requirements. This is an extremely important point, and one that many people do not seem to understand.

> It just doesn't make sense to sternly discipline kids in the 21st century for being 21st century kids.

Perhaps the bottom line is that you cannot keep or deter all students from using their phones at school. It is going to happen. You can therefore decide to be prohibitive or permissive. You can officially ban them from campuses, or allow them during certain times (or all times). Whatever you do, though, you will have to figure out a way to get students, educators, and parents on board, and probably approach it in a way that represents the climate you are trying to build and maintain. This climate should be all about encouraging the positive and responsible use of technology, and dissuading its misuse and abuse, and that should be fostered and facilitated as much as possible.

QUESTIONS FOR REFLECTION

When it comes to mobile device policies, do you think that you can start to move in a more permissive direction, instead of continually trying to fight the proverbial tide? How can you set a high standard, but encourage youth to rise to that standard—instead of expecting the worst from them in terms of their behavioral choices?

38

Fewer Schoolwide Bans on Devices, More School Climate Initiatives!

Sameer Hinduja

Computers have long been a fixture in many U.S. schools. Indeed, Justin and I had computers in our middle schools back in the 1980s. And when we visit schools today—large and small, rural and urban—they (of course) all have computers. Many schools have computer labs or general-access machines in libraries or other common areas. In addition, many classrooms have their own computer(s), and teachers regularly use various technologies to deliver educational content or enhance instruction. Some schools even provide laptops or tablets to each individual student ("one-to-one" schools). While there is some debate about whether these programs are worth the money, it is clear that technology is a big part of education. And computers have diminished in relevance in recent years, as we use our smartphones and iPads to do much of what we used to do on our desktops and laptops.

Some schools have attempted to prevent inappropriate technology use at school by simply writing a policy that prohibits students from bringing their devices to school.[49] Short of strip-searching students as they come through the front door, it is practically impossible to enforce a complete ban like this. Most administrators have largely conceded this point and therefore have enacted policies that say something to the effect of "If I see it, you lose it." Our colleague Mike Donlin, program supervisor for the School Safety Center in the Washington Department of Education, has quipped that schools should approach cell phones the same way they do underwear: "We know you have them—we just don't want to see them in class."[50] We believe a broad-stroke ban preempts opportunities that exist for students to use technology in positive ways. And there are many.

Allowing students to bring their devices to school holds much promise for furthering their education.[51] Most schools do not have enough resources to provide a laptop or tablet for each student, and since many already have a cell phone, tablet, or other portable device, few additional expenditures are required (e.g., the school can lend devices to the handful who don't own one). Teachers can ask students, once equipped, to research particular questions using their devices. They can use audience response systems via clickers or cell phone live polling to assess student competency with certain concepts. They can assign creative, interactive projects using the camera functionality and photo- or video-sharing sites. Many teachers use Facebook, Twitter, and even Instagram as supplemental instructional tools. Indeed, educators are even using the popular game Angry Birds to teach complicated physics principles.[52] The opportunities are as endless as the web itself. We have received many phone calls from administrators who are considering opening up their schools to student-owned mobile devices because of the headaches associated with attempting to keep them out and the positives that may accompany using them to help kids learn. According to a report published by Walden University, "Teachers who use technology frequently . . . report greater benefits to student learning, engagement and skills from technology than teachers who spend less time using technology to support learning."[53]

> Allowing students to bring their devices to school holds much promise for furthering their education.

While we clearly need to recognize the potential problems that may accompany the positives when students "bring their own devices" to school, it is important to stress that technology isn't the problem. There is nothing inherently problematic about cell phones; they are amazing devices that have revolutionized the way we communicate. Similarly, there is nothing fundamentally dangerous about Facebook, Instagram, Snapchat, or any new technology that comes down the proverbial pike. Social media use has allowed interpersonal relationships to start, restart, and thrive, generating many emotional and psychological benefits.

However, some will choose to use technological enhancements to cause harm to others or, intentionally or unintentionally, cause harm to themselves. This harm is often not physical—although there might be physical ramifications and side effects. Rather, it tends to manifest in less visible but possibly even more damaging ways. It is those behaviors that we should focus on—not the technology.

According to the Centers for Disease Control and Prevention, motor vehicle crashes are the number-one cause of death of teens.[54] In 2013, approximately 2,500 teens died in car accidents.[55] Does this mean we should ban teens from driving? Of course not. But we do need to take steps to prevent accidents from happening, such as providing driver's education classes, encouraging parents to model appropriate driving habits, establishing safety guidelines, and so forth. The same approach needs to be taken with technology. You wouldn't just throw your teenager the keys to the family sedan and say, "Good luck and be safe!" But this is often what we do with technology: we assume that children will be safe and smart because we tell them to do so (or because they must have heard and internalized all of the lessons from school and on the news!).

We need to be much more deliberate and comprehensive than that and regularly remind teens about issues they may run into. They are adolescents. How many times did you learn a lesson on the first go-around when you were a teenager? Probably not as often as you would like. Neither did we, so don't feel bad. This should serve to inspire us in the ways we deal with and instruct teens. Parents have to do this in their households, and we believe they bear the largest load when it comes to teaching their kids to use technology wisely. However, school personnel unquestionably share a good portion of the responsibility as well, since those kids are their captive audience for much of the day. Most schools now realize that they need to educate students about appropriate online behaviors and take steps to prevent students from misusing technology at school. Educators also know that what happens online—whether during school hours or on evenings and weekends—often directly impacts what happens at school. We constantly advocate that schools prevent cyberbullying and sexting by developing and maintaining a positive, respectful, and nurturing classroom and school climate.

We talk about improving school climate a lot because we believe in it, have studied the existing research about it, and have conducted research on it ourselves.[56] It matters, and it works.[57] The National School Climate Center defines school climate as "the quality and character of school life. School climate is based on patterns of students', parents', and school personnel's experience of school life and reflects norms, goals, values, interpersonal relationships, teaching and learning practices, and organizational

> A positive climate engenders respect, cooperation, trust, and a shared responsibility for the educational goals that exist in a school.

structures."[58] In general, a positive climate engenders respect, cooperation, trust, and a shared responsibility for the educational goals that exist in a school. Educators, students, and everyone connected to the school consequently take ownership of the mission of the school and work together toward a shared vision. If a climate like this is established, everything else seems to fall into place. For instance, it will definitely lead to more academic success and greater educational exploration. According to Daniel L. Duke, professor of education at the University of Virginia:

> *No one program, policy, or practice can address all of the reasons why young people harm themselves and others. No single strategy can prevent strangers or staff members from jeopardizing the well-being of students. The most prudent course of action for all schools is to address safety comprehensively.*[59]

We believe that there will be fewer behavioral problems at school and online, because students will not want to damage the positive relationships they have at school by doing anything that will disappoint or upset the educators or other students with whom they are strongly bonded. Ideally, sentiments expressed should sound something like this:

"I am not going to post that online—Mrs. Smith is my favorite teacher and is really awesome, and I don't want her to think badly of me!"

"I don't want my friends at school to think I am a moron for sending that message."

"I am totally going to keep my profile page clean, since everyone else at my school does it too."

"I don't want to miss out on any opportunities and fall behind my peers, so I have got to build a positive online reputation!"

"I don't want to stand out for doing the wrong thing when everyone else is doing the right thing!"

We know that teens are more likely to be deterred from engaging in inappropriate behaviors by a fear of how their friends or family members (or others in their lives they look up to) might respond than by adult nagging.[60] Indeed, we know from experience (and you will likely agree) that this deterrent effect is much stronger than prohibitive policies and laws (see Chapter 22). Therefore, by developing strong relationships between the school and students, among the students themselves, and between the school and the students' families, this principle can be used to dissuade negative behaviors and encourage positive behaviors even when adults aren't around—such as when teens are online.

QUESTIONS FOR REFLECTION

Since a positive school climate is such a strong predictor of so many desirable educational goals, what specifically are you doing to create and maintain such an environment on campus? In what areas are you deficient, and how can you correct them?

39

TEENS AND TECHNOLOGY

School District Policy Issues

Sameer Hinduja

One of the most important steps a district can take to help protect its students, and protect itself from legal liability, is to have a clear and comprehensive policy regarding bullying and harassment, technology, and their intersection: cyberbullying. Almost every state requires districts to have a comprehensive policy in place, which generally involves one (or more) of the following elements:

1. Requirement to add "cyberbullying" or "electronic bullying" to current anti-bullying policies

2. Provision of specific graduated consequences and remedial actions for bullying

3. Provision to allow administrators to take reasonable action when off-campus actions have affected on-campus order or the learning process

4. Requirement to notify parents/guardians

5. Requirement for counseling of targets and aggressors

6. Requirement to develop new investigative, reporting, and disciplinary procedures in bullying cases

7. Mandate that schools create and implement prevention programming (such as Internet safety, ethics, etiquette training, and curricula)[61]

For our book *Bullying Beyond the Schoolyard*, we fleshed out what we believe are the most important components of an effective school cyberbullying policy.[62] This stemmed from our research into what schools were currently doing, and what was working and not working. Apart from the aforementioned elements, we believe that tying bullying prevention and response to a more holistic initiative to improve school climate is most promising.[63] Let's explain further the elements that should comprise these policies, so you can make sure your school has solid footing before you deal with any incidents this year.

First, it is important that the policy clearly defines the behaviors it seeks to proscribe. The more specific the policy is, the more likely it will withstand legal challenges. As William Shepherd, a statewide prosecutor in Florida's Office of the Attorney General, cautions, however, "The law or policy should be specific, but behavior changes over time, so you must have the ability to grow with the times."[64]

Also, we list below several forms of bullying that should be clearly delineated in your policy. Generally speaking, any communication that a student perceives as unwanted, vulgar, obscene, sexually explicit, demeaning, belittling, or defaming in nature; that is otherwise disruptive to a student's ability to learn and a school's ability to educate its students in a safe environment; or that causes a reasonable person to suffer substantial emotional distress or fear of bodily injury should be subject to discipline.

FORMS OF BULLYING

Bullying can occur by one individual or a group of individuals, can be direct or indirect, and can take the following forms:

A. "Physical bullying"—demonstrations of aggression by pushing, kicking, hitting, gesturing, or otherwise invading the physical space of another person in an unwelcome manner, or the unwanted tampering with or destruction of another person's property

B. "Verbal bullying"—demonstrations of aggression through insults, teasing, cursing, threatening, or otherwise expressing unkind words toward another person

C. "Relational bullying"—demonstrations of aggression through exclusion, rejection, and isolation to damage a person's position and relationship within a social group

D. "Cyberbullying"—the intentional and repeated harm of others through the use of computers, cell phones, and other electronic devices

Cyberbullying can result in discipline whether it occurs on or off campus; whether it involves an electronic device at school, at home, or at a third-party location; and if it results in a substantial disruption of the learning environment as defined in the school's policy.[65]

It is also essential to remember that many districts already have policies in place that prohibit various forms of harassment, including harassment based on race or sex. Any behavior that constitutes sexual harassment, for example, should be handled under those provisions, irrespective of whether the behavior is also considered bullying or cyberbullying.

With regard to penalties, any student found to be participating in, contributing to, and/or encouraging acts of cyberbullying and/or harassment toward another student or staff member must be disciplined. Your policy must identify what specific actions will be taken. To determine the severity of the harassment or discrimination, the following may be considered: how the misconduct affected the education of one or more students; the type, frequency, and duration of the misconduct; the number of persons involved; the subject(s) of harassment or discrimination; the situation in which the incident occurred; and other related incidents at the school. Any cyberbullying that has been perceived as a criminal act, such as a threat to one's personal or physical safety, will be subject to discipline and result in the notification of law enforcement.

Discipline can include a number of different actions:

- Parental contact
- Behavioral contracts
- Loss of privileges (either in school or extracurricular)
- Conferences with students, parents, teachers, or administrative staff
- Interventions by school guidance personnel
- School service work or student work detail
- Removal of student from class
- Loss of bus privileges (parents are thus responsible for transportation)
- In-school alternative assignments or intervention programs
- Detentions (before, during, or after school, or on Saturday)
- Restitution
- Restorative practices
- Assignment to alternative program in lieu of suspension days
- Suspension—removal of student from school for up to 10 days

- Assignment to an alternative educational facility
- Expulsion—removal of student from school for remainder of year plus one additional year

We've discussed that it is critical to link specific behaviors with specific disciplinary outcomes so that students know exactly what may happen if they are caught engaging in cyberbullying behaviors.[66] Don't be afraid to think creatively about alternative sanctions instead of relying on detention or suspension. For example, those who cyberbully others could be required (based on the grievance) to research and write an essay on the negative effects of cyberbullying. They could also be required to write a formal apology to the aggrieved party or parties. Disciplinary outcomes should be considered and carried out on a case-by-case basis.

> We've discussed that it is critical to link specific behaviors with specific disciplinary outcomes so that students know exactly what may happen if they are caught engaging in cyberbullying behaviors.

We really think that you should be as specific as possible in your policy—make sure you cover harassment and cheating and disrupting the class environment by texting or Instagramming or Snapchatting, and talk about threats and explicit pictures and pornography laws and police intervention. Clearly outline the consequences for prohibited behaviors. Get students and parents in on this discussion. Schools will have problems as the school community gets used to these changes, but hopefully the problems will be few and far between and the situation will get better with time.

Students will learn appropriate behaviors, and these should—in time—become the norm if a positive school climate is prioritized and established.[67] For example, in the mid-2000s, phones were much more of a problem in our college classrooms than they are now. University students, at least in our experience as professors, have gotten better at phone etiquette and are not letting the devices distract them from learning. Sure, a phone occasionally will go off in class, but usually the student is apologetic and immediately acknowledges the faux pas. Of course, middle and high school students are different from those in a university, but we are optimistic that we can work through the same challenges at the secondary school level.

After a policy is created or revised, the school community needs to be educated about it. Students should be informed about the circumstances under which their personal portable electronic devices can be confiscated and searched. They should also be reminded that anything they do on a school-owned device is subject to review and appropriate discipline. This should be explained to students and parents, possibly through assemblies, orientations, community meetings, and messaging strategies (voice mails, memorandums, etc.). Be intentional about conveying these messages, and don't just assume they know your policy! As a student from Florida recently told me:

> I think it's a good idea that all schools include in their handbook definitions of the types of bullying and sexting as well as the consequences and/or disciplinary actions, but then perhaps kids should be quizzed on this every school year. Call me an airhead, but I never read the school's student handbook until my family moved to Florida my junior year of high school. I remember I got in trouble the first day of school because I clearly did not read the dress code part of the student handbook. My old school handed out agendas and handbooks at the beginning of the school year, but no one ever read them. Those things would just get stuffed at the bottom of our lockers. If all schools enforced something as simple as reading the student handbook and made sure students understand what they're reading, then I think they would be a step closer to educating kids that they can get help if they're being bullied.[68]

QUESTIONS FOR REFLECTION

Policies won't be the primary way in which bullying behaviors are prevented, but they need to be in place for accountability and to support disciplinary sanctions. How are you getting the word out to your student body about what specific behaviors are prohibited, and why? How can staff continually remind students about these rules without always preaching or lecturing about them? Finally, are consequences always following rule violations, or do some students sometimes get away with their behaviors? How can consistency be gained so that students don't think the school is a pushover, or unfair in the equal application of sanctions?

ENDNOTES

1. Sacco, D. T., Silbaugh, K., Corredor, F., Casey, J., & Doherty, D. (2012, February 23). *An overview of state anti-bullying legislation and other related laws*. Retrieved from http://cyber.law.harvard.edu/sites/cyber.law.harvard.edu/files/State_Anti_bullying_Legislation_Overview_0.pdf
2. San Diego Unified School District. (2016). DP Bully Report Form. Retrieved from https://www.sandiegounified.org/schools/de-portola/dp-bully-report-form
3. Family Educational Rights and Privacy Act (20 U.S.C. § 1232g; 34 CFR Part 99).

4. Hinduja, S., & Patchin, J. W. (2015, April). Using Google Voice for student reporting of bullying and cyberbullying incidents. *Cyberbullying Research Center*. Retrieved from http://cyberbullying.org/Google-Voice-Bullying-Reporting-System-for-Schools.pdf

5. You can find the video on YouTube (https://www.youtube.com/watch?v=x1lM6UgaOfI).

6. Yarbrough, B. (2014, January 22). Disturbing high school bullying video shows how real this problem is. *The Huffington Post*. Retrieved from http://www.huffingtonpost.com/2014/01/22/high-school-bullying-video_n_4644787.html

7. National Center for Education Statistics & Institute of Education Sciences. (2015). *Indicators of school crime and safety: 2014*. Retrieved from http://nces.ed.gov/pubs2015/2015072.pdf

8. Hinduja, S., & Patchin, J. W. (2015). *Bullying beyond the schoolyard: Preventing and responding to cyberbullying* (2nd ed.). Thousand Oaks, CA: Corwin.

9. Johnson, P. (2009, March 20). Final defendant in teen beating gets jail time. *The Ledger*. Retrieved from http://www.theledger.com/article/20090320/NEWS/903209978

10. You can find the video on YouTube (e.g., https://www.youtube.com/watch?v=sb1WywIpUtY).

11. Patchin, J. W., Schafer, J. A., & Hinduja, S. (2013). Cyberbullying and sexting: Law enforcement perceptions. *FBI Law Enforcement Bulletin, 82*(6), 2–5.

12. Ibid.

13. *Miranda v. Arizona*, 384 U.S. 436 (1966).

14. Caccarozzo, J. L. (n.d.). *Juvenile* Miranda *rights*. Retrieved from https://www.fletc.gov/sites/default/files/imported_files/training/programs/legal-division/downloads-articles-and-faqs/research-by-subject/5th-amendment/juvenilemirandarights.pdf; see also *J.D.B. v. North Carolina*, No. 564 U.S. ___ (2011). Retrieved from http://www.supremecourt.gov/opinions/10pdf/09-11121.pdf; *N.C., a Child Under Eighteen v. Com.*, 396 S.W.3d 852 (Ky. 2013). Retrieved from https://docjt.ky.gov/legal/documents/NC.Final.pdf

15. *New Jersey v. T.L.O.*, 469 U.S. 325 (1985).

16. James, R. K., Logan, J., & Davis, S. A. (2011). Including school resource officers in school-based crisis intervention: Strengthening student support. *School Psychology International, 32*, 210–224.

17. James, N., & McCallion, G. (2013). *School resource officers: Law enforcement officers in schools*. Retrieved from https://www.fas.org/sgp/crs/misc/R43126.pdf; McDevitt, J., & Panniello, J. (2005). *National assessment of school resource officer programs: Survey of students in three large new SRO programs*. Retrieved from https://www.ncjrs.gov/pdffiles1/nij/grants/209270.pdf; Thurau, L. H., & Wald, J. (2009). Controlling partners: When law enforcement meets discipline in public schools. *New York Law School Law Review, 54*, 977–1020.

18. Hinduja, S., & Patchin, J. W. (2013). Social influences on cyberbullying behaviors among middle and high school students. *Journal of Youth and Adolescence, 42*, 711–722.

19. City of Monona Code of Ordinances. (n.d.). Ordained and published by authority of the Common Council (p. 317). Retrieved from http://www.mymonona .com/documentcenter/view/422

20. *Davis v. Monroe County Board of Education*, 526 U.S. 629 (1999); *Davis v. Monroe County Board of Education*, 120 F.3d 1390 (11th Cir. 1997).

21. Geis, G., & Binder, A. (1991). Sins of their children: Parental responsibility for juvenile delinquency. *Notre Dame Journal of Law, Ethics & Public Policy, 5,* 303–322.

22. Office of Juvenile Justice and Delinquency Prevention. (1997). *Juvenile justice reform initiatives in the states: 1994–1996.* Retrieved from http://www.ojjdp .gov/pubs/reform/ch2_d.html

23. *In re: Mariah T. v. Monique B.*, 71 Cal. Rptr. 3d 542 (Cal. Ct. App. 2008). Retrieved from http://caselaw.findlaw.com/ca-court-of-appeal/1190445.html

24. *Lewis Caldwell v. Louis Zaher*, 344 Mass, 590 (1962). Retrieved from http:// masscases.com/cases/sjc/344/344mass590.html

25. Tyler, J. E., & Segady, T. W. (2000). Parental liability laws: Rationale, theory, and effectiveness. *The Social Science Journal, 37,* 79–96.

26. Quoted in Sutton, J. R. (1981). Stubborn children: Law and the socialization of deviance in the puritan colonies. *Family Law Quarterly, 15*(1), 31–64.

27. McCluskey, C. P., Bynum, T. S., & Patchin, J. W. (2004). Reducing chronic absenteeism: An assessment of an early truancy initiative. *Crime & Delinquency, 50,* 214–234.

28. Personal communication, June 13, 2013.

29. McCluskey, C. P., Bynum, T. S., & Patchin, J. W. (2004). Reducing chronic absenteeism: An assessment of an early truancy initiative. *Crime & Delinquency, 50,* 214–234.

30. Tucker, J. (2008, January 18). Free speech and "cyber-bullying." American Civil Liberties Union: Speak Freely. Retrieved from https://www.aclu.org/blog/ speakeasy/free-speech-and-cyber-bullying

31. *Tinker v. Des Moines Independent Community School District*, 393 U.S. 503 (1969).

32. *Bethel School District No. 43 v. Fraser*, 478 U.S. 675 (1986).

33. *Davis v. Monroe County Board of Education*, 526 U.S. 629 (1999); *Davis v. Monroe County Board of Education*, 120 F.3d 1390 (11th Cir. 1997).

34. *J.S. v. Bethlehem Area School District*, 757 A.2d 412 (Pa. Commw. Ct. 2000).

35. *Wisniewski v. Board of Education of the Weedsport Central School District*, 494 F.3d 34 (2d Cir. 2007).

36. *Barr v. Lafon*, 538 F.3d 554 (6th Cir. 2008).

37. *Lowery v. Euverard*, 497 F.3d 584 (6th Cir. 2007).

38. *Kowalski v. Berkeley County Schools*, 652 F.3d 565 (4th Cir. 2011).

39. See *Emmett v. Kent School District No. 415. 92* F. Supp. 2d 1088 (W.D. Wash. 2000); *J.S. v. Blue Mountain School District,* 650 F.3d 915 (3d Cir. June 13, 2011); *Klein v. Smith*, 635 F. Supp. 1440 (Dist. Me. 1986); *Layshock v. Hermitage School District*, 593 F.3d 249 (3rd Cir. 2010).

40. *Layshock v. Hermitage School District* , 593 F.3d 249 (3d Cir. 2010) (en banc). Retrieved from http://www2.ca3.uscourts.gov/opinarch/074465p1.pdf; *J.S. v. Blue Mountain School District,* 650 F.3d 915 (3d Cir. 2011). Retrieved from http://www2.ca3.uscourts.gov/opinarch/084138p1.pdf

41. *New Jersey v. T.L.O.*, 469 U.S. 325 (1985).

42. *Klump v. Nazareth Area School District*, 422 F. Supp. 2d 622 (E.D. Pa. 2006).

43. *J.W. v. DeSoto County School District,* No 09-00155 (N.D. Miss. Nov. 11, 2010).

44. Ibid.

45. See also Cyberbullying Research Center. (2011, July 7). *Bring your own device to school.* Retrieved from http://cyberbullying.org/bring-your-own-device-to-school

46. Cyberbullying Research Center. (2011, August 8). *Cell phone search checklist for school administrators.* Retrieved from http://cyberbullying.org/cell-phone-search-checklist-for-school-administrators

47. Personal communication, September 1, 2011.

48. *No Child Left Behind Act of 2001*, Pub. L. No. 107-110, 115 Stat. 1425 (2002), 20 U.S.C. 6301 et seq.

49. Hinduja, S., & Patchin, J. W. (2015). *Bullying beyond the schoolyard: Preventing and responding to cyberbullying* (2nd ed.). Thousand Oaks, CA: Corwin.

50. Cyberbullying Research Center. (2009, August 13). *Cell phones at school and student expectation of privacy.* Retrieved from http://cyberbullying.org/cell-phones-at-school-and-student-expectation-of-privacy

51. Cyberbullying Research Center. (2011, June 1). *Formal rules for students and their devices at school.* Retrieved from http://cyberbullying.org/formal-rules-for-students-and-their-devices-at-school

52. Muyskens, K., & Grundmeyer, T. (2014, September 4). Teach physics with Angry Birds. International Society for Technology in Education. Retrieved from https://www.iste.org/explore/articledetail?articleid=147

53. Grunwald and Associates. (2010). "*Educators, Technology and 21st Century Skills: Dispelling Five Myths.*" Walden University. Retrieved from https://www.waldenu.edu/masters/ms-in-instructional-design-and-technology/highlights/five-myths

54. Centers for Disease Control and Prevention, National Center for Injury Prevention and Control, Division of Unintentional Injury Prevention. (2015, October 14). Teen drivers. Retrieved from http://www.cdc.gov/motorvehiclesafety/teen_drivers/

55. Insurance Institute for Highway Safety & Highway Loss Data Institute. (2013). *Teenagers.* Retrieved from http://www.iihs.org/iihs/topics/t/teenagers/fatalityfacts/teenagers

56. Hinduja, S., & Patchin, J. W. (2012). *School climate 2.0: Preventing cyberbullying and sexting one classroom at a time.* Thousand Oaks, CA: Corwin.

57. Hinduja, S., & Patchin, J. W. (2015). *Bullying beyond the schoolyard: Preventing and responding to cyberbullying* (2nd ed.). Thousand Oaks, CA: Corwin.

58. National School Climate Center. (2016). What is school climate and why is it important? Retrieved from http://www.schoolclimate.org/climate/

59. Duke, D. L. (2001). *Creating safe schools for all children.* Upper Saddle River, NJ: Pearson.

60. Hinduja, S., & Patchin, J. W. (2013). Social influences on cyberbullying behaviors among middle and high school students. *Journal of Youth and Adolescence*, *42*, 711–722.

61. Hinduja, S., & Patchin, J. W. (2015). State cyberbullying laws: A brief review of state cyberbullying laws and policies. *Cyberbullying Research Center*. Retrieved from http://cyberbullying.org/state-cyberbullying-laws-a-brief-review-of-state-cyberbullying-laws-and-policies

62. Hinduja, S., & Patchin, J. W. (2015). *Bullying beyond the schoolyard: Preventing and responding to cyberbullying* (2nd ed.). Thousand Oaks, CA: Corwin.

63. Hinduja, S., & Patchin, J. W. (2012). *School climate 2.0: Preventing cyberbullying and sexting one classroom at a time.* Thousand Oaks, CA: Corwin.

64. Personal e-mail correspondence, September 2, 2012.

65. Hinduja, S., & Patchin, J. W. (2015). *Bullying beyond the schoolyard: Preventing and responding to cyberbullying* (2nd ed.). Thousand Oaks, CA: Corwin.

66. Hinduja, S., & Patchin, J. W. (2011). Cyberbullying: A review of the legal issues facing educators. *Preventing School Failure: Alternative Education for Children and Youth*, *55*, 71–78.

67. Hinduja, S., & Patchin, J. W. (2012). *School climate 2.0: Preventing cyberbullying and sexting one classroom at a time.* Thousand Oaks, CA: Corwin.

68. Personal communication, December 5, 2010.

Index

A SAGE Publishing Company

Helping educators make the greatest impact

CORWIN HAS ONE MISSION: to enhance education through intentional professional learning.

We build long-term relationships with our authors, educators, clients, and associations who partner with us to develop and continuously improve the best evidence-based practices that establish and support lifelong learning.

Solutions you want. Experts you trust. Results you need.